LEAVING THE PAIN BEHIND

A Piece of Prison Life

Joshua Roberson

NEWMAN SPRINGS PUBLISHING
320 Broad Street
Red Bank, NJ 07701

First originally published by Newman
Springs Publishing 2023

All biblical citations were taken from the New
International Version of the Holy Bible.

ISBN 979-8-88763-540-8 (Paperback)
ISBN 979-8-88763-541-5 (Digital)

Printed in the United States of America

Mother,

I dedicate this book to you. Ever since I was in prison, you had been there right by my side. I know we have been through a lot over the years, but you never looked back at the past. You taught me how to love and how to forgive. You showed me how to keep my faith. When I wanted to give up after I came to prison, you were there telling me to keep on trying, because God is in our midst.

If it wasn't for you, and the faith God put in you, I would be lost, and I wouldn't know what to do. I'm glad that I have a praying mother, and all your prayers brought me through. No one can take the love that I have for you away from me. And when it's all said and done, it was you who kept me strong through Jesus Christ.

Mother, I thank you for all that you have done for me. When I didn't listen to you, you still were there. Don't ever think that you are to blame for my stupid actions. It was my choice; you did all you could. Once again, I thank you, and I thank God for you. I wouldn't trade you for anything in the world.

You are one of the greatest gifts that God has given me other than life. And when I cry at night, I think about the love that we share. When you gave me a hug during your visit in the prison, I really didn't want to let you go. I felt safe in your arms. So I dedicate this book to you, and I want to say I love you always and forever. One more thing: you have never let me down. Thank you.

Love, your son,
Joshua Keith Roberson

INTRODUCTION

The mind, it's a powerful and unique tool. The mind can be dangerous if you're not careful. Don't ever let your mind control you, but you control your mind. Your mind can put you in a place where there's no place to run or hide. Your mind can make you feel like you're doing right, but you know you're doing wrong. Those are the types of games your mind plays if you let it.

The mind is an element or complex of elements in an individual that feels, perceives, thinks, and wills. The mind holds memories and applies knowledge. The mind dreams of things you can't even imagine. The mind is an organized conscious and unconscious adaptive mental activity of an organism. The mind is a principle of intelligence. The mind can play mind games such as a psychological tactic. The mind can be foolish as well as have a purpose and goals. Like I said before, the mind, your mind, is more powerful than you think.

Your mind can put you in a prison that no key can open. Your mind can make you feel like you have a life sentence without parole. The mind can treat you like a slave. The mind at times can make up its own law. I love the way Paul said it,

But I see another law at work in the
members of my body, waging war against

the law of my mind and a prisoner of the
law of sin at work within my members.
(Romans 7:23)

My name is Joshua K. Roberson, and I was born in Houston, Texas. I lived in Houston all my life. I decided to write this book because there are some things people needed to know. And maybe by hearing my story, you can discover that key to freedom of life. This book is designed to help you and me on how to *leave our pain behind.* This book will teach you to break free from the *prison mind,* because you can be in prison in your mind and be trapped in this world knowing that you have no place to go. So let's come together and take that stand so we can and will *reverse this curse!*

I've been in the prison mind all my life. I know that sounds confusing, but it's true! It took me to come to an actual prison to learn how to be free from the prison mind. Even today I'm still struggling to break free. As I'm writing this book, it's not just to help the readers, but also to help myself find that freedom of life. We can help each other.

I hope you'll enjoy the poetry that expresses my deepest thoughts and feelings. Who knows, it might just help you come out of a prison you're going through. I know I can't save the world; however, if I can only just save one and help them out of captivity, that is all that matters.

You don't have to be religious to read this book. You can either believe in God or not, and you can still find yourself trapped in a prison mind with no escape. I'll pray that if you don't believe in God, you'll seek him. Because I know he's the only one that holds the key and can help you break free.

I deeply encourage all handicapped and disabled people to continue to follow their dreams. I believe and I know God has a gift for each and every one of you. Today is the day to discover that gift. I know there will be times you will feel like you have to give up, there will be times you will think life just can't go on, and there will be times you find yourself hopeless, with no faith at all. But I am here to tell you, just believe! Don't let your thoughts captivate you into that prison mind. It's time to be set free.

Finally, the stories that will be told are based on truths. The names of the people and places in these stories have been changed to protect their identities.

The scripture you'll be reading is coming from the *Life Application Study Bible NIV.* This book has some inappropriate language.

So sit back, relax, and learn, as I open the doors of the adventures of my life!

CHAPTER 1

Born Different

When I was born,
I was born with a disability.
My mother and father didn't know why
    this happened to me.
I have wondered each and every day, why
    God made me this way?
I didn't have any friends,
But the Lord knew I wanted my life to
    end.
I have missing body parts,
My mother used to always tell me,
"Don't worry about what people say
    because you're God's work of art."
When I got to elementary,
The children were all making fun of me.
They laughed and they joked.
This was the pain I had to go through
As I have fallen and have soaked in my
    tears shaking in fear!
I have three sisters and one brother, and
    none of them were made like me.

I started thinking,
"Was I someone else's child?
Could it be a possibility?"

Now I'm feeling empty…

The Birth

June 22, 1985, I, Joshua K. Roberson, was born. You would think when people have a newborn they will be filled with joy. My parents' story was different.

My mother, Linda M., was only twenty-one at this time. She couldn't believe this was happening to her. This probably was the worst experience my mother ever experienced in her life at this time. She was so young and didn't know how to handle it. Prior to my birth, my mother had two other children: my eldest sister, Kelly M., and my second eldest sister, Kim R. They both were born without any problems. So why was I?

My father, Felipe R., was about twenty-seven years old. People said you couldn't tell how he felt about my birth. He showed no emotions, as if he was emotionless. I believed he just didn't want my mother to worry. So he had to stay strong and be there to support my mother in whatever decision she decides to make.

You see, I was born with one hand and one foot. I have half of fingers on my right hand, and I had a cleft lip. When I did get my color, I was brown skinned, I had black hair, and I had big eyes. I was a healthy baby, but I was just born different.

Do you know God won't put more on us than we can bear? (1 Corinthians 10:13). My mom tried to believe that, but Satan knows how to attack young people. So my mother did the only thing my grandmother, her mother, taught her how to do, which was to pray.

Pain

Pain, it's an experience that we all go through. Pain, it's something most of us, if not all of us, don't like. Pain, it's a feeling that we can't stand. So why does God allow us to have pain? What does that word truly mean?

Well, *Merriam-Webster's Dictionary* tells us, "Pain causes distress; to hurt, trouble, and grief." Also, pain can irk or annoy or be otherwise troublesome, like the phrase "pain in the neck." That's just to name a few. That's the world we live in today. We allow pain to take over our lives, but we ask ourselves that question, why?

Pain is a type of prison a lot of us see ourselves in. We wonder why God allows this stuff to happen. Can we be free from fear? 2 Timothy 1:7 says,

> For God did not give us a spirit of timidity, but a spirit of power, of love and self-discipline.

As you read about Peter in Matthew 14:22–33, it talks about when Jesus told his disciples to get into the boat and go ahead of him so he can dismiss the crowed after feeding the five thousand. Later that night Jesus was walking on the lake. His disciples saw him walking on the lake, and they thought he was a ghost. So they cried out in fear. Jesus immediately said, "Take courage! It is I don't be afraid" (Matthew 14:27).

So Peter said, "Lord, if it's you, tell me to come to you on water." Jesus replied, "Come." As Peter got out of the boat and walked on water, toward Jesus, he saw the wind. He was afraid. He began to sink. So he cried out to the Lord, "Save me!" Jesus immediately caught him and said, "You of little faith, why did you doubt?"

The meaning of this story is that it wasn't the wind that Peter was afraid of; it was the lack of trust in God. He took his focus off God, and his faith became little.

My mother was afraid; she had fear of taking care of a disabled child at a young age. She took her focus off God and allowed Satan to attack her mind. Let's stop focusing on Satan's lies and start focusing on God's Word. If you take your focus off God for just a second, you will find yourself sinking, just like Peter. As I end this chapter, I'm going to leave you with this:

> I am still confident of this: I will see the goodness of the Lord in the living. Wait for the Lord; be strong and take heart and wait for the Lord. (Psalm 27:13–14)

CHAPTER 2

The Birth Part 2

My mother was always a Christian, but her faith wasn't where it needed to be…

The days when my mother was in the hospital, family and church members of my parents were frequently visiting. They were filling my mother's head up by telling her to give me up for adoption. They told my parents the reason God allowed this to happen was because both my parents were living in sin by not being married. The church people told my mother she was too young to handle a situation such as this.

The doctor went as far as telling my mother I was going to be mentally retarded, and I wasn't going to be able to talk, walk, or think for myself. My aunt Ruth, who is my father's sister, didn't want to pick me up. My mother was hurt and confused. Her faith was wavering back and forth between her circumstance and God's promises.

My mother wanted to find that faith line so she could step across. But she was weak, was young, and didn't know whom to believe. My father and my mother's mother stood by my mom's side the whole time. My mother prayed and prayed, and God delivered her. That's when she said, "I'm taking my son home!" That's what was told to me. But her faith was still a little weary. The reason I said that was because I was told that my mother said, "If I have another child, and if he or she becomes disabled, I will give them up for adoption."

How many of you today are wavering your faith back and forth between your circumstances and God's promises? We as people always look at our situations instead of God's promises. I am here to tell you God's promises never fail. No matter what you're going through, keep the faith, and watch God work in your life.

That reminds me of Abraham in the Bible, whom we need to be more like. God promised Abraham that he was going to be the father of many nations, even though Abraham was a hundred years old and he knew his wife, Sarah's, womb was just as dead as he thought he was.

Abraham's faith wasn't weak. He obeyed God and waited until God fulfilled his word.

Abraham never doubted God. Even though he was under direct pressure, he still believed. Yes! God did fulfill his promise. Abraham is the father of many notions, and the entire world was blessed by him. Jesus is our promise. He died for our sins so we may live again. All you have to do is have faith in him and believe. Then you will see miracles start to take place in your life. So I encourage you to cross that faith line just as Abraham did. You can read more of Abraham's story in Genesis 12:1–25:18.

I was four years old now, and my mother had my little sister Brazil R. It's 1989; my parents were married now. Thank God Brazil was born with all her limbs. So was it true what the church folks said? When I was born, my parents were not married, now they were, and Brazil came out just fine. So why was I cursed? That's the question.

We lived in the city, Houston, Texas, to be exact. We had a three-bedroom house in a small black community called Carverdale. To me, it was more like living in the country. In my neighborhood, there were a lot of trees, few houses, and farm animals.

Everyone in Carverdale just about knew each other. My uncle Jeff and my aunt Belinda lived next door to us with their kids, Starr and John R.

Our house was built on two lots. We had a three-car port garage and a washroom. We also had an 8x8 dog cage behind the washroom with two dogs, Rocky and Starr. So you can say we had a pretty big yard.

Being only four years old, my relationship with my parents was okay. My dad didn't baby me much; but with my mom, on the other hand, I was her star. With regard to the relationship with my siblings, I can say we got along. By looking at them, I knew something was different. See, Kelly was tall, slim, and brown skinned. She was pretty. Kim was about seven, dark skinned, slim, and also pretty. They say Kim looked more like my dad than my mom. I also have a brother, but he didn't live with us. He lived with my grandmother, who was my father's mom. They lived in Carverdale as well. My grandmother—we call her Big Momma—lived two streets down from where we stayed.

My brother—Ken R. is his name—was tall, dark skinned, and handsome. He was my father's child. My father had him before he met my mother. Ken was born with all his limbs, and he also was the eldest.

I was closer to my mother than my father. Maybe the reason was because she was the one who was taking me back and forth to the hospital because of surgeries. One minute the doctors were trying to fix my fingers, keeping them from sticking together. The next minute they're fixing my cleft lip.

Even though I was only four, I was starting to feel pain, emotional pain. I was seeing my sisters and my brother do everything, while I felt like I was left alone. I know my family loves me, but I just couldn't see it. That's what a prison mind does to you. My prison mind started at the age of four. I was trapped, and I couldn't get out. I remember when I was about five or six, I would cry for no reason. Truth be told, there was a reason. Satan started to attack me. Even though I was young, he found one of my weaknesses. My pain started to grow. Since then, the piece of that experience has stuck with me.

Let me talk to the handicapped and disabled people for a minute. Have you ever felt alone? Do you believe no one cares? Are you going through some pain, emotional pain? Do you feel like God isn't there? I have some news for you. Don't ever give up on God when you're feeling lonely. Satan knows when God has a blessing for you. So he's going to do everything in his power to get your focus off God so your blessing can be held up. Stop feeling sorry for yourself. Trust me, I know. Feeling sorry for myself almost destroyed my life.

When I was six, the game I loved was beating on things. You name it, I was beating on it. I wasn't just making noise; I was making music. I discovered one of my gifts. I remembered my parents used to always yell, "Joshua, stop all that damn noise!"

I couldn't; it was in me.

CHAPTER 3

Pain

As you read in chapters 1 and 2, my mother was desperately seeking for answers. So she did the number one thing my grandmother thought her how to do: pray! Now let's see what the Bible tells us about pain.

The Bible says, "Pain is physical, mental, or emotional sufferings." My mother was hurting from the outcome of my birth. It wasn't too much of the physical pain or the mental pain.

She was suffering from a lot of emotional pain.

Emotional pain can be just as bad as if you fell off your bike and skinned your knee.

That's called physical pain. In some cases, emotional pain starts the process of all the other types of pain. How so? Well, I'm glad you asked!

When you're hurting emotionally from whatever that caused your pain, like a bad breakup, a death in the family, or your child being born disabled, you start to hurt inside. It hurts to the point that you can't take it anymore. Then comes your mental pain. It has you thinking about all kinds of crazy things. It will get you to that point where it will drive you crazy, and now you've just had a nervous breakdown. Here comes the physical pain rearing its ugly head. Since you passed the emotional and mental stage, now your body starts to hurt or have headaches and heartaches, or maybe even your eyes are giving you problems. Do you feel me? Am I making any sense? I'm sure after my mother dealt with her emotional pain, the thought of the mental pain came next, followed by the headache she may have had through the physical pain.

So where does pain come from? God pointed me to the beginning of the Bible, the beginning of the creation of man, in Genesis.

We all know the story about Adam and Eve and how they disobeyed God. The world was without sin, without pain; but because of our lack of knowledge, we wanted to be just like God by knowing good and evil. Adam and Eve didn't realize that their disobedience was going to cost the world.

It was a painful experience Adam and Eve faced by disobeying God. This is what God said to the woman,

> I will greatly increase your pains
> in childbearing; with pain you will give
> birth to children. (Genesis 3:16)

And to Adam God said,

> Cursed is the ground because of
> you; through painful toil you will eat of
> it all the days of your life. (Genesis 3:17)

Satan is the enemy. He will try to destroy you at all costs. Satan's plan is for us to doubt and question God. "Why, Lord? What have I done to deserve this?" Sounds familiar? Satan also wants us to be discouraged, to look at our situations so we can take our focus off God. Now Satan wants us to defeat ourselves, making us feel like we are nothing and making us give up.

The day I was born I believe my mother had doubt, I believe she was discouraged, and I believe she almost defeated herself. But she never gave up on me. She took me home. Even though I was young, I had doubt. Then I started to feel discouraged. The day I started looking at my sibling, I felt like I didn't belong.

I believe pain can have beneficial results as well. You see, pain, just like sorrow, joy, anger, or love, is a source of energy. Like all energy, pain's effect depends on how we use the energy. Physical pain is designed to let us know there's something wrong with a certain part of our body. How far would medicine get without the age-old question "Where does it hurt?"

Emotional pain may seem like a negative thing, which it can be. But in fact, one of its purposes is to cause us to see the beauty in life. If you're in a relationship, for example, and you get badly dumped, the next time you'll be more careful about who you let in your heart. Plus, if it works out, you'll appreciate it that much more. Not dealing with pain can also be very destructive.

Another example: I have a friend named Blake. He had a twin brother named Ryan. Ryan was shot in the chest and was killed. The perpetrator was never caught. Blake was hurt, but instead of dealing with his pain and grief like a healthy human, he ran from it. He turned to heroin and alcohol. He was absolutely miserable, and the whole day was devoted to numbing himself. Eventually he made a series of decisions that led him to an aggravated sentence in prison.

So you see, if Blake had dealt with his pain in a healthy way, he wouldn't be sitting in prison today. That is that prison mind I am talking about. In the prison of heroin and alcohol,

Blake allowed these things to trap him in a prison mindset. Pain overtook him.

Don't allow things that happen in your life form into a prison mindset you can't get out of. If you feel pressured, get on your knees and pray. God will set you free.

Is there a way for us to *leave our pain behind*? Adam and Eve messed up their relationship with God. They thought their way was better than God's way; at times we believe that our way is and will be the best way. They hid; don't you hide sometimes from God when you know you've done wrong? They had too many excuses, like some of us today.

Today you can *reverse this curse* and start on the process of *leaving your pain behind*. First, you should stop trying to defend yourself of your wrongdoings and excuses. You must learn how to accept your punishment for what you have done. You should stop playing hide-and-seek with God. Have you ever heard of the saying "You can run but you can't hide"? Stop trying to hide from God; you won't win! Then finally, you have to see that God's way is the only way. Just let God handle it!

CHAPTER 4

The Delivery Room (A Short Story)

June 22, 1985, Houston, Texas

"Push, push, push!" a man's voice was yelling. That's all she could hear, people yelling, sweat dripping from her face. She's in pain, as if a bus just hit her from behind. Bright lights, people in blue like paper gowns. Their faces had masks on them. The pain was getting worse by the minute.

Now here came a head coming out of her.

"Ahhh!" La'Tasha J. screamed. So many voices, too many tools, as if she was being tortured by Satan's demons. It was unreal. But she recognized one person, her boyfriend, Timothy W. He was standing at the side of her bed holding her hand yelling, "Baby, you can do it! You're almost there. Come on, push!" He also was in pain caused by the numbness in his hand from La'Tasha squeezing the hell out of it.

"There's a problem," one of the doctors said. "We have to get him out of there, now!" Tasha and Timothy started looking around, trying to see what was going on.

"Baby, what's wrong?" La'Tasha said worried, while she was still pushing and breathing very heavy. Tim let go of Tasha's hand, and he headed over to the other side of the bed where one of the doctors was standing.

The look on Timothy's face was very unhappy. "Doc, what's going on?" The doctor didn't respond.

"Doc—" Tim was interrupted.

"Mr. Wright, your son is wrapped around in the umbilical cord. If we don't get him out now, he could die!" the doctor said.

Tim went back over to the other side of the bed where he was standing and grabbed hold of Tasha's hand. "Tasha, everything is going to be okay. I promise," he said with a concerned look on his face.

The doctor grabbed the child's head gently and pulled until he came out crying. What a relief it was for La'Tasha, but she knew something was wrong with her son.

The Hospital Room

You can hear a woman crying, lying in her hospital bed, tears falling from her eyes, shaking her head in disbelief. La'Tasha couldn't believe after carrying her newborn son, Isaiah W., for nine months, two weeks, and three days that his birth would be a problem. After having two kids prior without any problems, she just couldn't understand this situation.

There he was, lying in his mother's arms, eating from his bottle.

It was a long day for Isaiah, you know.

The doctors amputated his left hand and amputated his right foot. His fingers weren't long enough; they were like little nubs. The only good thing he had was his thumb. Did I mention he had a cleft lip?

As Tim was standing beside La'Tasha's bed, he leaned over to kiss her on the forehead. She looked into his big brown eyes and gave him a depressing smile, as she was wiping the tears from her face.

"Why, how could this be?" Tasha said, looking down at her son, Isaiah, trying to hold back some more her tears. "I did everything that I was supposed to do. I have two kids, so why this one?" Disappointment started to rise in her voice. Tim grabbed Tasha's hand; he was trying to contain himself.

"Baby, everything is going to be okay," Tim whispered. La'Tasha turned her head from him. "Tasha, Tasha, baby, look at me," Tim was still whispering. Tasha slowly turned her head back toward Tim.

Tim picked Isaiah up from his mother's arms. "It's okay, don't worry," he said.

"What the hell do you mean 'it's okay'? You promised everything would be." Tears were flowing from her eyes. Anger was now in the room. "I don't know if I can do this. I'm too young!" She began to question God.

"Stop, stop this right now!" Timothy's voice was in distress. "What the hell is wrong with you? This is our child, and we're going to love him the same way we love our other children. So get yourself together." Tim left the room with Baby Isaiah in his arms.

La'Tasha needed some answers, so she closed her eyes, and she began to pray.

Broken Heart

Listen to my words
And hear my sighs.
Listen to my voice
And hear my cries
In the morning at sunrise.

Are there arrows that I'm following
          through?
The shadows of my pain,
A heart that is broken into pieces,
Will it ever be able to regain?
I am soaking in my sorrows
Like there is no hope or joy for tomorrow.
Through all the things
That life can bring,
Will my broken heart ever be repaired
Through the separations and all of the
          frustrations
And must I say rejections?
A heart that needs to forgive
So, my soul will forever live.
As I'm sitting here watching the world go
          by.
There are tears in my eyes
Because I'm hurting deep down inside,
And I refuse to lose everything that I've
          gained,
And the world can keep all or its fame.
As my mind becomes weak,
Is it love that wants to seek?
I've tried and I've tried to renew my
          strength,
But through it all I have to believe I got
          the hint.
What about my broken heart?
Can we transform it into God's work of
          art?

Delusion

My heart is beating.
My pulse is pounding.
My knees are weak.
I dropped to my feet.
I don't know what's going on.
All I can hear is the end of tone.
Sweat dripping into my eyes.
My mind it's institutionalized.
Do I have the same identity and the abil-
    ity of a mind of creativity?
Do I have an identical twin?
Going through the same thing,
Trying to hide within?
I don't know who I am.
I don't have any identification,
Nevertheless, no memorization.
I'm starting to see things aren't there.
Could it be a guardian angel flying in the
    air?
I'm so exhausted, I feel like I got executed
    by lightning.
My life is so frightening that I hear voices
    telling me to do things.
Things I don't want to do such as,
"Kill yourself, hurt others,
And make them feel the pain like you're
    going through."
I've been pushed off the face of this
    nation.

The world is a new illustration.
I've fallen into this deep black hole.
What is this I see?
People souls are surrounding me and
    screaming at me.
They want their souls to be set free,
So, I awake.
This is the life I don't want to take.
I'm losing my mind.
Is this a sign of confusion of a man that
    is delusional?

No Limitations

What comes to mind at this present time?
When your life is being controlled by the
    anxiety of your fears?
Looking in the mirror on the flip side
    trying to hind
So, you can cover up the reflection of
    your tears.
Staring directly into the future not know-
    ing where your life is about to go.
Watching the world passes by as our gen-
    eration starts to grow.
We have been put in sloppy places,
And I see the reaction on peoples' faces.
Life is like a dream that goes away in the
    morning.
There's violence in every dark corner of
    the land. We set no limits on earth
    for man to understand.

We walk through the waves crossing the
    deep sea
Trying to find the promised land
So, our souls can dance free.
It's hard to explain the mysteries from the
    past,
The images in our heads will for-ever-last.
Ever since we were young, we've suffered
    from the pain,
All the long they surrounded us like a
    flood from the rain.
As we closed our eyes and realized the
    intensity that we have within us,
We can explore the world exactly the way
    the world should be.

No disrespect life isn't perfect,
Eventually it will come around to that
    day we have to stand on the founda-
    tion of destruction.
Don't be surprised
When you have to stand on your own
    two feet
And your life has been circumcised
As you're burning up in the heat.
Let's make a commitment and confess
    with an agreement
That there's no excuse for us to be this
    loose.
This is the rhythm of no limitation!

The Battles of Life

As I go through the battles of life.
I have to face the struggles, the hustles,
    and the ups and downs, but through
    it all I have to say,
"I'll do it for you."
My life is aching from the pain.
I see your tears through the rain.
Help me, Jesus; I'll do it for you.
I hear your voice through the thunder,
As my life began to wonder.
Guide me, Lord Jesus, as I fight on this
    battlefield.
Protect me with your shield.
My enemies are healthy and strong.
My heart is pounding, my strength is
    almost gone.
Everything that I see
Tells me not to believe. My past tries
    to control me. Will this hurt ever
    leave?
I made some mistakes that were painful.
And some situation I run into that wasn't
    helpful.
It's so hard living day by day trying to put
    up my guard,
But through it all I have to say,
I'll do it for you.

CHAPTER 5

Dying Inside

Dying inside is when your body shuts down on you emotionally. Dying inside is more of a mental or emotional death. When you die inside, it's like you're losing all hope. Dying inside will make you become lonely, hopeless, distressed, or helpless. I felt like I was dying inside from 1992 to 1996. I was in so much pain. My prison got me to the point where I wanted to give up everything, even my life.

In 1992, my family and I were still living in Carverdale. About this time, the neighborhood had more houses and fewer trees, but we still had the farm animals. Carverdale became a friendly neighborhood; everyone got along and helped those who are in need.

I was seven years old, and a lot has changed with my body. The doctors came up with a way for me to walk and use my left hand. I had a prosthetic leg, and I had a prosthetic arm that was shaped like a hook. It was very hard for me to get used to, but at times I believed I'd managed.

I was brown skinned, I had black hair and brown eyes, and I was slim. I had a deep scar on my right lower hip caused by the bone the doctors took out to fix my cleft lip.

At this time, I believe I was from another planet because I looked different from the rest of my family. My relationship with my parents was very quiet. I know my mother and father loved me, but they never sat me down to talk to me to see if I had any questions about my birth.

My parents never knew how much pain I was in since I was four.

I really encourage parents today to talk to their children on a daily basis, because you don't know what your child is going through, unless you sit down with them and listen. I wish I could start my childhood over, and maybe I wouldn't be where I'm at today.

My relationship with my elder sister Kelly was okay. When she was about twelve years old, Kelly made sure all of us were taken care of. I was so stuck in my own ways I didn't let her know what was really going on with me. The relationship with my other sister Kim was distant. I don't know what her problem was; she didn't get along with me anymore.

I didn't have a relationship with my brother Ken. He really never came around. As a child, I didn't know why. So not being around my elder brother hurt me too.

Being born different, I started to blame people for everything, even if I knew it wasn't their fault. For example, I thought my brother never came around because of me. He didn't want to be seen with his "freak" brother. Kim, I always thought she was mean to me because I wasn't like the rest of my siblings. And my parents, I thought they never sat me down to talk to me because they really didn't care for me. In my mind, I believed they only loved me because that was the right thing to do.

My prison mind was growing. I was trapped in this place, and I don't know which way to go. Be real with yourself: do you blame others for your problems? As a child, I was very confused, but now that I'm older, I can see clearer. I wanted protection, and I didn't know where to get it from. Now I believe my family was trying to give me that protection, but I refused it.

CHAPTER 6

Elementary

In 1992, I was going to Sleep Elementary in Banks ISD in northwest Houston. I can remember my first year of school like it was yesterday. I was so excited to start first grade, but I didn't know it was going to cause me so much pain.

On my first day of school, I was scared. My heart felt like it stopped and dropped down to my ass. I couldn't feel my legs; they were numb. My eyes were watery, and my throat was dry. The excitement that I was feeling passed right through me.

My mother dropped me off in front of the school. As I got out of her car, the numbness went away, and my eyes dried up. As I entered into the front doors of Sleep Elementary, I walked to the main hallway. I froze. My eyes started wandering. Something was really different.

I felt out of place.

Do you feel out of place sometimes? Could it be some place you know? Or could it be a place you feel like you just don't belong? That's the way I felt for two reasons: First, none of the kids were missing any limbs. So now I really felt like a person from another planet, like Mars! Second, most of the kids in the school were white. So I was thinking, *What the hell is going on here?* The day just couldn't get any worse.

Now that I thawed myself out, I headed toward the cafeteria to see what classes the counselors had enrolled me in. Walking the school grounds, I can see the kids looking at me, staring at me, even laughing, and joking. Some I heard saying, "He's such a freak." Tears started falling from my eyes. I'd never been "put down" before. That day I was, and it was very hurtful.

Finally, I entered the cafeteria. I dried my eyes. I headed toward the counselors' table. I can still see everyone staring at me, as if I was some type of unknown species. When I approached the counselors' table, there was a white woman sitting on the other side. She was blond-haired and blue-eyed with nice teeth and freckles on her face.

I was staring at her; she's staring back at me. Then she said, "What is your name?" I didn't respond. So she repeated it, "Son, what is your name?"

"Joshua R.," I mumbled to the point where she couldn't hear me, or so I thought. The woman opened a brown folder full of papers. She pulled out one sheet that had my name on it.

She handed it over to me. She smiled and pointed me toward the direction I needed to go.

When I got to the place where I needed to be, I looked at the sheet of paper the counselor had given me. It was my schedule, but I knew something was wrong with my schedule. I was thinking, *I'm already a freak, and now I'm an idiot!* The counselors enrolled me in special education classes.

Fear

I was not scared anymore. Why? Fear took over. This was the day, the first day of school, I allowed fear to take over my life. Even though I was young, I believed in God, or should I say my parents taught me about God? Did I really believe? I knew how to pray because I had seen the people do it at church every Sunday. I was hurting, lonely now, and I knew it was going to be hard to make friends.

How many of you today let fear take over your life? You could have been young or up in age, but fear found a way to creep in. So now you're letting fear control you. You have no place to run or no one to turn to. Let me offer you a solution. Listen!

> When I am afraid, I will trust you.
> (Psalm 56:3)

David wrote this part of the Scripture when the Philistines had seized him in Gath.

David is trying to teach us how to trust God's care in the midst of our fears. When you feel like dark clouds are covering you, there is still one truth that shines so bright. If God is for us, those people who are against us will never prosper.

I know that I was young, but if I had the Scripture taught to me, maybe I would have had something to stand on back then. The kids in my school were mean to me, and they embarrassed me. Yes, it affected me to where I formed another type of prison mindset, the prison of fear from people and fear of trusting them. Have you ever asked yourself this question, "What can people do to me?" Maybe they can cause pain, cause suffering, or even cause your death.

But what I've learned throughout my adventures in life is no one can steal your soul.

Fear can be very powerful; don't ever let it override your logical thinking or produce different types of behaviors.

> Trust in the Lord with all your heart and lean not on your own understanding. (Proverbs 3:5)

Eventually I realized that my parents were very good to me, but sad to say, they didn't teach me fully how to trust in God. I was afraid, scared, and lonely. No matter if you're young or old, trust in God in every decision you make. Pray and God will lead you and guide you and make your paths straight by protecting you. All I wanted was that protection, and I felt like I didn't get it.

Don't ever overestimate the power of fear and underestimate God's power. Isaiah 40:29–31 says,

> He gives strength to the weary and increases the power of the weak. Even youths grow tired and weary, and young men stumble and fall; but those who hope in the Lord will renew their strength. They will soar on wings like eagles; they will run and not grow weary; they will walk and not be faint.

God's strength is the key to our strength. When you feel like life just can't go on, call upon God, and he'll renew your strength. God's power and strength will never fail. The next time you fear, fear God who controls your life, and the afterlife.

Throughout first grade, I didn't have any friends. But I finally met someone I can call a friend. At this time, I really didn't trust him. His name was Jasper B. He lived in the same neighborhood as I. Jasper was brown skinned, was short, and wore glasses. Jasper also went to Sleep Elementary. The reason I didn't trust him was because I had already made up my mind that I couldn't trust anyone.

My mind formed that prison of fear of trusting. Jasper had never done me wrong, and he always took up for me when the other kids were picking on me. Because you form a prison mind of fear of trusting or whatever you may be afraid of, you don't let people get close to you, even if they have been there by your side through it all. You see, that is what traps you. Someone has done you wrong so much that when another person who really cares comes along, you block them out. For example, how did your mother and father treat you when you were young? Your parents could have treated you like they didn't love or care for you. They blamed you for their problems. They told you all the time they wished you were never born! That's painful. They may even knock you around a bit so you will have trust issues. Or you may have had a friend who has done you wrong. Now you can't trust anyone who tries to get close to you.

You may have been raped or molested as a child. The pain was so deep that you can't trust anyone who tries to be with you or tries to be your friend. Your mind has formed that prison of no escape. Now you're facing the prison of fear or trust. Don't let it control you or destroy you. Some people let their prison mind of fear affect them so much they even stop trusting in God. I could have lost my best friend Jasper a long time ago because I was an asshole to him when we were young. Jasper was a true friend. He stayed by my side through it all.

I'd been called all kinds of names in first grade. Because I had a prosthetic arm that was shaped like a hook, everyone was calling me Candy Man and Captain Hook. I felt so help-less and hopeless. At times it got so bad that Jasper couldn't help me. I let that entire stuff ball up inside of me, and that's what was killing me mentally and emotionally. There were times I had to cry myself to sleep. Being only seven, I didn't know people can be so mean.

My cousin Starr also went to the same school. She didn't help me much. The reason being, back then, just like it is now, kids had self-images to protect.

The only thing that calmed me was my favorite sub-ject, music! Playing music, hearing music, that was my peace. Music helped my pain and suffering go away.

Before I get into the next chapter, remember this, par-ents, please communicate with your children daily so they will know what's going on in life. Kids, trust your parents and let them know if you have any problems. This is for everyone; trust God because he is your strength when you are weak!

CHAPTER 7

Dying Inside

Dizziness is my name.
My body isn't the same and pain is the
    game.
This is unusual for my body to feel the
    way it feels.
It's getting too personal for my body it
    doesn't want to heal.
I can't describe my organs; it's getting
    hard as a brick.
My body is getting weak, and my stom-
    ach is getting sick.
My heart is pumping blood, but the
    blood is full of mud.
As the needle goes into my vein, I am
    going insane because the bugs still
    remain.
My lungs feel like clay and all I can say is,
    damn, why do I feel this way?
My brain is just like water, it's going right
    through me.
I'm praying to myself and hoping that
    this is just temporary.

I'm thinking, *How can this come about,*
    and when is this feeling gonna come
    out? My bones are covered in tissue.
I'm trying to figure out the issue.
Is this an instruction or limitations
    of an experience or maybe even
    maintenance?
I feel a chill like ice on top of a hill.
Can this be a symbol of patterns of colors?
I don't want this to go any further.
This is like a disease running through me
    like antifreeze.
I'm feeling a squeeze, I'm running out of
    air, and I'm losing my hair.
It's like my body is running a circus and
    my mind can't focus.
My body is causing confusion and my
    eyes are playing delusional games.
My tongue is rotating; my nose has sores
    and everything inside is separating.
Am I dying inside?
I don't know, well it's time for me to go.
I
Am
Out
Of
Here!

Dying Inside Part 2

There were people standing around me in the cafeteria. I didn't know what was going on. My mother was sitting on one side of me, and my father was sitting on the other side of me. I started looking around, and I noticed people I had never seen before dressed up in suits. Then as I turned toward the door, I saw the news cameras entering. Out of nowhere, I started crying. My mother put her arms around me. For some reason, I was frightened.

Minutes later, a woman stood in front of us at the podium. She was slim, about 5'9", and black haired. Her name was Ms. Lockheart. She was my special ed teacher at Sleep Elementary.

"Excuse me, can I have everyone's attention please?" Ms. Lockheart said with a smile on her face. Everyone in the room began to quiet down. "Today we are here to honor a very special student of mine. I noticed last year when he was in first grade, he was having problems writing. As you all know, he was born with a disability." Ms. Lockheart was staring at me with a smile.

That's when I realized she was talking about me. My heart started beating fast. More tears started to fall from my eyes. I grabbed hold of my mother's arms; I squeezed them tight.

"It's okay, son," my mother said in a low voice.

Ms. Lockheart continued speaking. "When I saw the special child, he won my heart. So I'm glad to say that my family and I will love to donate one of the first Apple computers to him. This computer will follow him throughout his school years until his writing improves. Now put your hands together as I welcome up Joshua R."

Everyone started clapping. Ms. Lockheart motioned me to come up. I was shaking my head while I was saying, "No, no, no!" As I was crying louder and louder, my father got out of his seat and grabbed my right hand. Ms. Lockheart walked over to where I was sitting and grabbed my left arm; they both pulled me up out of my seat and walked me to the podium. I wiped my eyes, and one of the men wearing a suit was standing at the podium. He stuck out his hand, and I shook it.

Ms. Lockheart was one of the teachers who influenced me the most. She tried so hard to make my life comfortable. Being only eight, it was too late. My prison mind had gotten worse. I was still being made fun of. One day I found myself not only liking girls, but also liking boys. I formed once again another prison mindset, which was homosexuality.

My family and I went to Greater Macedonia Baptist Church (GMBC); my uncle was the pastor. We had been going to GMBC ever since I was about three. I know God. I know he created me. What I didn't know was why God made me such a mess. Was he in a hurry? Or did he just run out of time? That's what I was asking myself.

In 1995, the school district zoned Carverdale to Banks ISD. Now every young person on the neighborhood was going to Sleep Elementary. Later that year, I was at school on the playground. Several kids were mean to me, but I believe they went too far. I was standing over by the monkey bars. A group of kids approached me and pushed me down. They took off my prosthetic leg and started playing Keep Away from Josh. I got up and started hopping after them. I was so hurt, and no one was there to protect me. Where was Jasper? Where was Starr? Where was Ms. Lockheart? Hell, where was God? It got to the point where I was just about to throw in the towel and give up.

That evening after I got off the bus, I ran into my house and grabbed a knife. I took the knife outside, and I walked to the middle of my driveway. With tears falling from my eyes, I was pointing the knife to my chest. Then my cousin Starr saw me from next door. She ran from her yard to mine and screamed, "Josh, what in the world are you doing!" She was screaming very loud. I didn't respond. As soon as she got to where I was in my yard, she held out her hand and said, "Josh! Give me the knife." She was panicking.

"I can't take this anymore," I said, crying harder. "I'm sick of people making fun of me. Maybe the world would be better off without me." Starr took the knife out of my hand. Then she started crying. Starr wrapped her arms around me, and we began to pray.

Have you ever been in a situation such as this? Have you ever wanted to take yourself out because of the pain, hurt, or depression? What I learned about myself is that I really didn't want to kill myself. I really wanted the attention so people can notice me. I prayed, but I felt like God didn't want to answer me. I could have hurt myself inside the house, but instead, I took the knife outside so people can see me. I just wanted to know if anybody cares. If you feel the way I felt back then when I was a child, pray and don't give up on yourself or on God.

David is telling us in Psalm 13:1–5 we must continue to trust God and not give up when he doesn't answer us immediately. David was also telling us it's okay to express your feelings to God. David was in distress. You can tell in verses 1 and 2 when he kept saying, "How long?"

> How long, O Lord? Will you forget me forever? How long will you hide your face from me? How long must I wrestle with my thoughts and every day have sorrow in my heart? How long will my enemy triumph over me? (Psalm 13:1–2)

When I was a child, I was asking God those same questions. It seems like every time I prayed, God didn't respond.

Do you feel that way at times? How many of you know God's time is not our time? That doesn't mean for you to give up. That just means to be patient.

David claimed that God was slow to act on his prayers. You know, we today often feel the same impatience. When bad things happen to us, we wonder when God is going to step in. In times of your despair, have faith. It is hard to hold on than to give up. If you give up on God, you give in to all of your problems. If you have patience, God's time will be on your side.

The same year I tried to kill myself was the year my sister Kim and I got into a fight. Kim tried to flush my head down the toilet. She dragged me to the bathroom, then she put my head inside of the toilet, and she tried to drown me in toilet water. Come to think of it, it's funny now; but the day that it happened, I was terrified, hurt, and troubled. Later that same year, my elder sister Kelly ran over my head with her bicycle. Now you know there are two sides to each story. If you let Kelly tell her side of the story, she will say that she told me to lie down on the ground, and then she ran me over. The real story was that Kelly was chasing me with her bicycle. I tripped over a rock and *bam*! Kelly couldn't stop in time, and she ran me over. Either way, I was badly hurt.

The year 1995 wasn't good. First, I tried to kill myself. Then my sister Kim tried to drown me, and Kelly ran over my head. By the end of the year, I believed my parents formed a prison mind of their own. They started fighting and arguing. There wasn't a day that went by my parents didn't fight. It was very hard for me and my sisters to deal with my parents' mess. The cops were always coming over; there was the breaking of stuff. As a child, it could really be damaging.

Faking Emotions

Do you ever try to fake your real emotions? What I mean is that you pretend to feel one way, but deep down inside you feel another way. When I was young, I faked my emotions a lot.

One of the reasons I faked my emotions was so my family wouldn't think I was sad because of the way I was born. I pretended to be happy; but deep down inside I was upset, depressed, angry, and mad as hell. Another reason was so my mother wouldn't feel guilty of thinking I blamed her for my birth.

If you asked any of my family members about me, they would tell you when I was young, I was just the happiest little kid ever. That would be a lie. I was confused, asking myself, *Why in the world was I born different from the rest of my family?* I had to hide my emotions so people wouldn't know how I really felt. I came a long way by faking my emotions. My family and friends looked up to me. They see me with a physical disability, and they know I didn't let it stop me from what I wanted to do. I pretended to be happy as if my disability didn't matter to me. Yes, it did matter! My disability messed up my childhood. By faking my emotions, it didn't make it better. I held in so much pain and sorrow it trapped me into a prison mind I couldn't get out of.

If you do fake your emotions, that's not really a good thing. Now when I try to tell my family and friends how I really feel, it's not believable. What I mean is that every time I express my real feelings, someone always says, "Naw, you're stronger than that." That's the hurt I have to go through because they look up to me as a stronger person. Faking your emotions could eat you up to the point where you can form a prison mind.

CHAPTER 8

Losing Myself

Remember in chapter 6 when I said, "Don't ever let your fear override your logical thinking or produce different types of behaviors"? Well, throughout my early grade school years, that's exactly what happened. It really started when I was in fourth grade...

The Act of Fear and Anger

There I was sitting around a table with four classmates in art class. The teacher gave us a project to do. While doing this project, because fear of being around people already took over my life, I hit this girl in the eye with my hook.

"Okay, class," the teacher said, "today I want you all to draw a picture of your family. Use as many colors as you can. I put markers in the middle of your tables. So let's get to work."

Everyone started grabbing the markers of their choice. The first color I grabbed was a blue marker because it was my favorite color. I started drawing my mom, my dad, and my sisters. Right when I was about to draw myself, a classmate named Brandy took the marker out of my hand.

I stared at her for a minute.

"Give that back!" I said loudly.

"Give that back," Brandy imitated, mocking me in a baby voice.

"No! I want to use this marker." Now I was about to cry. "Wait until I finish using it," I said.

Brandy looked at me with an evil look and said, "I'm using it. And anyways, my mother said we're supposed to get what we want when we want it. By the way, you're a freak."

Just that instant, I thought about all the years people used to make fun of me and picking on me. I thought about the fear and the anger. I looked at my prosthetic arm, and before you know it, I hit Brandy in the eye. Blood was coming down from her eye. The other children jumped out of their seats. The teacher looked like she was going out of her mind. I couldn't believe I'd just done that. Now I was sitting in the principal's office...

I let fear and anger override my thinking and produced a behavior that got me into trouble. Here is another situation.

In fifth grade, I was sitting in computer class. I just got done with my work. I didn't think it would be a problem playing a game on the computer while the other children were finishing their work. The teacher, Ms. Willson, came up behind me and grabbed my shoulder. She stuck her nails into my skin and picked me up out of my seat. She threw me into the wall. I was scared and frightened. The other children were just staring. I'm sure they were frightened too.

Ms. Willson looked at me with an evil eye and said, "What are you doing?"

I didn't respond, but once again I had a flashback of all the people who pushed me around. I thought about all the children who took my prosthetic leg from me and played Keep Away. I saw an opportunity, and I took it. After Ms. Willson let me go, I turned around and grabbed the chair that was right next to me, and I hit Ms. Willson in the middle of her back. She screamed, and then I ran. The principal couldn't find me for like an hour. When they finally found me, I was in so much trouble it wasn't even funny.

The outcome of this story was that Ms. Willson got into trouble for putting her hands on me. And I let fear take over my life to the point where I lost all hope. Why did God allow this stuff to happen to me? What have I done to him? That's what I was thinking.

You see, fear could make you do things that you'll have regrets afterward. Fear can also make you have lack of trust, feel ashamed, feel guilt, and have thoughts of revenge. A lot of us have memories of some type of abuse. Don't let it control you. I really regret hitting Brandy and Ms. Willson. I just had a lot of rage and anger built up inside of me. Ms. Willson and Brandy were okay, and that was a good thing.

Out of Place

The day I started feeling out of place was that day I realized I was different from everyone else. I wasn't out of place just at home, but I was out of place from the rest of the world. Life was very hard for me. I was dying inside, and it was killing me mentally and emotionally. I was tormented, unappreciated, and mistreated. I didn't think God was on my side. Do you feel that way at times? Do you feel violated, ignored, and offended? Do you wonder where God is through your troubles? Have you lost all hope? I know as a child it has messed me up going through what I went through.

I didn't want to show any sign of weakness, so I didn't let anyone know how I felt. That tore me up inside the most. Keeping all pain hidden deep down inside made me felt very uneasy. If you ever felt or feel the way I did when I was young, don't hold it in. Talk to someone.

If you don't, that's what creates the process of dying inside. You'll form this type of prison mind that will trap you deep down inside with no escape.

Jasper and I became good friends. We always had a lot of sleepovers. I remember one night when Jasper stayed the night at my house and we saw something that blew our minds. We were in my room late one evening. We heard some noise coming from the living room area. We left my room and headed toward the living room. When we got to the living room, we stopped in surprise. We saw two or three unknown creatures. All kinds of thoughts started going through my head.

The next thing I knew, I woke up in my daddy's van, and Jasper was gone. I was alone. I don't know how I got there. Now was this just a dream? Because even today Jasper will tell you that never happened. How did I get into my daddy's van when the entire house doors were locked, chain and all?

I had a lot of crushes on girls when I was young. I can remember this one crush that I will never forget. I was in fifth grade, and there was this girl named Hanna. It was like I was in love the very first time I saw her. She was so beautiful. Hanna was tall and had a nice-shaped body, pretty light-brown eyes, and a wonderful smile. One day she noticed me staring at her.

So she walked over to where I was standing and said, "What are you looking at?"

I was speechless. I was so stunned I couldn't even breathe.

"You like me?" Hanna asked. All I could do was nod my head.

"Awww, that's sweet," Hanna said as if she was pleased.

Before you know it, she humiliated me in front of the entire school. Now I knew for sure I lost all hope in girls, in love, and in trust.

Losing All Hope and Peace

If you start to feel like you're losing all hope and peace, remember to trust in God. Have faith while you turn up your hope! Romans 15:13 says,

> May the God of hope fill you with
> all joy and peace as you trust in him, so
> that you may overflow with hope by the
> power of the Holy Spirit.

Meditate on God's promises until the picture becomes easily visible inside of you where nothing can break it out of you.

CHAPTER 9

Easing Pain, Overcoming Adversity

Here is a story of a young man who found himself trapped in a prison mindset. Not only was he giving up on life, but he gave up on faith, and he was giving up on God. It took him to come to an actual prison and be diagnosed with something that can end his life for him to turn back to God. God is the only one who can ease his pain. Here is his story.

*****

My name is Brandon Lewis, and from the moment I was born, my life consisted of hard times. My mother was disabled, and at that time, she had three other children. Many of my family members died back-to-back. My mother had two more children while the two elder brothers went to jail. I became the man of the house at the age of seven. Throughout the years depression, loneliness, anger, and many other negative things inhabited my mind. I wasn't able to work. I was taking care of my siblings. My family was very dysfunctional. I was always trying to assist my mother because she needed the help. Life was hard, but around ten when I left the house, I hung with the wrong crowd. I just wanted to feel loved and wanted attention.

A few years later, my family and I were homeless, panhandling to get food for the night, sleeping in shelters; and when all else failed, we slept in our car. Due to all the things I experienced, I became a prisoner in my mind. I was trapped in a mindset of "I'm nobody," "I'll never be anything," and so on. I became my own worst enemy. Despite having opportunities at college football, I declined wanting to help my mother. My mom died in 2005 from kidney failure; again I was homeless. A young lady I had been friends with for a few months accepted me into her home.

A month or so later, I found out she was pregnant. It turned out to be my son. To make a long story short, in 2007, I was charged for causing her death. I ended up in prison with a forty-year sentence. I was mad at God because I had prayed constantly for help, and by me being stupid, a beautiful young mother's life no longer existed.

In August of 2008, I was diagnosed with cancer (chronic myeloid leukemia). The pain and events of the years in an actual prison so far are indescribable. As much as I hate that I'm in an actual prison for this charge and that I'm battling cancer, God has brought me to my knees. I am truly saved now, and I want to live for God always. Things were a process, but I am who I am today by being in an actual prison. In the midst of the indescribable pain, God gave me a new life. I'm more at peace with myself.

I achieved my GED, I got into college, and I have completed many Bible and rehabilitation classes. None of this would have happened first without God's grace and strength.

And to the people God sent to encourage me that "I can" achieve my goals. Even though I caused a great misfortune, I know that I am still somebody. I freed my mind from putting myself down, and I am now confident in Jesus Christ. I am a gospel artist and a minister of God. I have one proposed ministry and three proposed organizations. I am still continuing to fight the good fight of faith. I am letting God ease my pain, while I overcome adversity.

Note: Brandon Lewis died from chronic myeloid leukemia in 2014 at one of Texas's prisons. May God be with his soul.

Out of Place

I feel like
I just don't belong here anymore.
Why do I feel so much pain and sorrow,
Like my soul is sore
Like some helpless kid?
I had a hard childhood,
So, I figure adulthood would be easier,
But it's not.
I'm trying to see my future,
But it's blocked
By my blind spot. I can accept that life is
      a b———
And it's unfair.
It only gets harder,
But I can't accept the fact that people
      expect me to care.
It is what it is!
Is it bad that I have no hope?
Will it get better?
Is it bad that I'm content with my life
Even though I feel so *out of place*
Like my life is tryin' to erase?
Is it wrong to be happy
With my messed-up life?

I'm so used to bad things following me.
This can't be a part of me!
Is it wrong to cry
When I feel weak?
It is wrong to be tired?
I'm tired of letting go of stuff
But still holdin' on to it.
This can't be me.
I know I sound crazy,
But I just feel *out of place*,
Out of touch with me.
I'm just ready to settle down for anything
Other than what I have now.
I want so much to be happy
And smile for no reason
I hate at times that I feel weak
And that I have to hide.
I feel like no one is on my side.
I want someone who won't let go
And let me fall flat on my face.
I'm tired of bein' *out of place*! I need
        someone to make the bad good
And the good great.
Or at least try,
With no lies.
I'm so lost
And it's scary,
But I hate it and love it
All at the same time.
Sometimes I think I'm unlovable,
Undesirable,
Tainted, because I'm so damaged
By life.

Why Do We Judge?

Let us look deep into our lives.
Sit back and rewind way back into time.
Over the mountains and hills,
Beyond the trees and fields, even over the
    ocean,
And deep down into the sea,
We as people look at others as a target
    device.
Aim, shoot, and fire negative feedback
    that isn't nice.
We are so caught up into our own evil
    darkness
We have so much hatefulness in our
    hearts,
We're lost into our own little town
Making fun of one another and putting
    each other down.
We are too busy killing each other's spir-
    its instead of raising them.
Some people don't want to hear it.
Can I be real,
And tell you how I really feel?
We judge each other because we feel low.
No place to hide and nowhere to go.
We as Christians—ha, don't let me go
    there.
We act like we have never been caught up
    in any evil affairs.
Jesus once said, "He who is without sin
    among you let him throw the first
    stone,"

But some of us won't leave it alone.
Let's try looking at what's on the inside
Instead of on the outside and see what
    blessings may come about.
When it all comes down to it,
Why do we judge?
Or should I say,
Who are we to judge?

A Cry for Help

There are forty thousand homeless peo-
    ple in the world,
And most of them are little boys and
    girls.
Why is it that we won't help these people
    that are in need?
But we hide like God made them the
    world's bad seed.
Is this the way it's supposed to be?
When Christ died on the Cross to set us
    free?
Free, huh?
We don't give a helping hand, and most
    of us just don't get it,
Or we won't understand.
Little children are dying on the streets,
With very little clothes,
And no shoes on their feet.
Is this a cry that lies beneath their skin,
As they weaken
And their bodies are getting thin?
Babies are getting sick

As their arms and legs are skinny as a
    stick.
All they wanted is the love from God
    given by his Grace,
But instead, we close the doors in their
    face.
We know that most teens are pushed into
    taking care
Of his or her little brother and sister
Each and every day,
But it's hard to see them eat out of the
    trash cans
In the streets where it stands.
This is sad; so sad that they wish they
    had what we have.
So, the next time you think life isn't fair,
Take a look back at those children
That don't have anyone to care.
All they can live on is faith alone.
This is a cry for help!

CHAPTER 10

The Family

Let's talk about my father's side of the family for a minute. My father had three sisters and one brother. His sisters' names are Ruth, Sarah, and Alexandra, whom we called Aunt Alex. My father's brother's name is Jeffrey, but we call him Uncle Jeff.

I'm closer to my father's side of the family than my mother's side. I love hanging with Big Momma, who is my father's mother. I will go to her house just about every day after school. Being in the state of mind as I was, hanging with my Big Momma kept me straight most of the time. Just about everyone on my father's side of the family is into music. Maybe that's where I get my passion for music.

My aunt Sarah is married with two children, Mary R. and Jack B. My aunt Ruth and my aunt Alex are not married or do not have any children. My uncle Jeff is married to my aunt Belinda, and they have two children, Starr and John R. My aunt Alex is the godmother of my little sister Brazil, and my aunt Ruth was the godmother of my cousin John. My aunt Ruth passed away in the year 2017.

I wasn't too familiar with my mother's side of the family. Even today I'm still not. I'm not for sure why or what was the real reason I wasn't close to my mother's side of the family.

My mother has one sister, Karen J., and one brother, James M.

I never really spent time with my mother's mom. My eldest sister, Kelly, always hung around my grandma than the rest of her grandchildren.

My mother's parents were divorced as long as I can remember. My father's parents had been together until my grandpa died, I believed, in 2005.

Note: My mother's parents passed away between 2009 and 2013.

CHAPTER 11

Unfold

When I was twelve years old
My life started to unfold.
I had a lot of friends,
Doing my own thing living in sin.
I realized the gifts God gave me:
Playing instruments,
Writing poetry,
Creating music.
By the time I was in the eighth grade,
The decision was already made.
My parents had filed for a divorce.
I was mad at God and very angry deep
    down inside.
I was full of sorrow
Like there's no hope for tomorrow.
This opened up a new emotion for me,
    my mind and body became sore.
I was moving back and forth
Between both parents and finally settling
    down with my father.
My life during this time wasn't stable.
I thought God couldn't put my family
    back together.

My family wasn't the same,
And also, I felt like I was the one to
blame...

Unfold

In 1997, Carverdale had grown rapidly. Everywhere you turn new homes were built. The people in the neighborhood got along for the most part. Banks ISD had a program in Carverdale called the Reading Program. This was a free program to help children get prepared for the TAAS test, which is called today as the STAAR test. When we were young, my sisters and I attended the Reading Program.

The relationship with my parents was still the same. I was a mother's baby, and my father still did most of the punishments when it came to us getting into trouble. Now don't get me wrong, my mother did some punishing too. My relationship with my sisters was very crazy. Kim and I still didn't get along. And Kelly was just the big sister. But what was so awesome was my little sister Brazil and I became best friends.

Troubled Marriage

By the time 1997 came around, my parents' relationship with each other got worse. Every time my parents were together, they're always fighting. Cops were always called to our home. The nosy neighbors were always looking. I felt like my parents' prison mind trapped them into a state of arguing, confusing, and falling out of love with each other.

We always went to church, but my mother's commitment on religion wasn't as serious as it should have been. I don't know much about the problems my parents were in. All I knew was my mother stayed out late and went to the clubs all the time. My father didn't like that. As for my father, I really don't know why my mother was always mad at him. Yes, there are two sides to each story, but the madness wasn't just on my mother.

My parents fighting really hurt our family. Every time they fought, it was so frustrating. I can't really speak for my sisters, but I know they had to feel the same way too. When my parents fought, it was embarrassing. The neighbors were looking and pointing at us while the cops were frequently at our home.

Watching my mother pointing a knife at my father was very frightening. Even though we knew my mother wasn't going to hurt our father, just witnessing my parents fighting was painful. I never saw my father hit my mother; maybe he pushed her a little bit. Can you imagine watching your parents acting like fools? Or can you imagine letting your children see you acting like fools?

If you are calling yourself a Christian, you should live on God's Word. Paul mentioned this about Christian marriage in 1 Corinthians 7:27, "Are you married? Do not seek a divorce." Paul is telling us that if you are married, you will face many troubles in this life (1 Corinthians 7:28). That does not mean for you to get a divorce!

Paul is letting us know many people think marriage is all gravy and it will solve all of their problems. If you think that, well, you're wrong! Marriage won't solve your loneliness, your sexual desires, your satisfaction of your spouse's emotional needs, and life's difficulties. It is your commitment to each other and your commitment to Christ that will help you through your conflicts and problems with your spouse.

Marriage is a wonderful thing, but marriage can't automatically fix every problem. It doesn't matter if you're married or single; you must stay focused on Christ, not on your spouse.

To read more on Christian marriage, you can find it in your Bible in 1 Corinthians chapter 7.

I believe my parents couldn't solve their problems because they took their focus off Christ. Getting a divorce can really affect your children's lives. Or even letting your children watch or hear you and your spouse fight can harm them. Not only are you putting yourself in a prison mindset, but you're forming a prison mind for your children. And if you ask me, that's not fair to them. So keep your eyes on Christ and let him guide your marriage. Then you'll see things turning around for the good.

Nothing really had changed about me during this time. I still looked the same. The only difference was I didn't have my hook hand anymore. The doctors made me a hand that looked real. This hand had fingers, and it opened and closed, and I did get taller. Now that I had this new hand it was cool, but I felt more and more like a robot.

I still never shared my feelings with anyone, not even Jasper or my little sister Brazil, and they were my best friends. I was trapped in this dark place, and I couldn't get myself out. My prison mind just kept me into a no-ending maze.

CHAPTER 12

In 1997, I started sixth grade at Clear Junior High School in Banks ISD. I had a heavy load to carry from elementary to junior high. What I mean is that I didn't talk to anyone but Jasper and Starr. I was already nervous and scared to enter the sixth grade. This can happen to you if you're in the prison mindset as I was or still stuck in the past.

Forever Changed

I was still in special ed class, and I still felt ashamed. But what I do remember about Clear Junior High School that changed my life forever was the day I was getting off the bus and I entered the cafeteria. As I was walking to the cafeteria line to get my breakfast, a beautiful light-skinned girl came up and walked beside me. She was a half-breed. When we got to one of the lines, she constantly stared at me.

I was thinking to myself, *Oh, Lord, here we go again.* Something was different about this situation.

"Hey, what is your name?" she asked. She was smiling at me. She was so pretty and gorgeous. All I did was stare back at her.

It wasn't the fact that I was scared or afraid; I was self-conscious and insecure about myself. And I wasn't going to get hurt again like when Hanna hurt me in fifth grade.

"Hello, what is your name?" she repeated. Once again, I didn't say anything, then she grabbed her tray and left.

Every day, the same half-breed girl would come up to me and ask, "What is your name?"

And every day, I wouldn't answer.

Three months after school started, I was sitting at the cafeteria table by myself eating my lunch. Something told me to look up, so I did. I felt gleaming eyes staring at me. So when I looked up, there she was, the same half-breed girl smiling with her tray in her hands. I took a deep breath, and I rolled my eyes, and I looked back down at my tray.

She asked, "Can I sit with you?"

I looked back at her, and I shrugged.

Without asking again, she sat down across from me at the table. She was still smiling at me. I looked at her with a disgusted look. I continued eating my food.

She asked again, "Hey, what is your name?" She never stopped smiling.

I was saying to myself, *This girl is really bothering me.*

I replied, "If I tell you my name, would you leave me the hell alone?"

She laughed. "Well, it depends."

I looked back at her, looking at her pretty smile and her wonderful teeth. "My name is Joshua."

"Nice to meet you, Josh. My name is Tiffany." She grinned. "It took you long enough to realize I just wanted to be your friend." We both laughed.

Ever since that day, my life changed. My life began to unfold at that very moment. I just couldn't believe how much my life had changed. I had a lot of friends. I finally fit in. About a month later, Tiffany and I started dating. I was in love with her. She helped me come out of my comfort zone.

With all the friends I had, I would have done anything to keep them. But I just couldn't come out of my prison mind.

*****

Since my little sister Brazil became my best friend, we did everything together.

Everywhere I went, she went. A lot of big brothers wouldn't like their little sister following them.

I was different. It made me feel good that my little sister looked up to me. She was so beautiful. Brazil was a yellow bone, had sandy-colored hair, and had pretty eyes; and for an eight-year-old, she was about medium height and medium build.

There was this man who lived across the street from my house, and his name was Mr. Jackson. He was an older man, and he liked when the kids from the neighborhood came over to his house to keep him company. I used to grab a trash can from the street and turned it over to beat on it. I would take the trash can to Mr. Jackson's house and beat on it while I got the other kids to sing gospel songs.

Mr. Jackson had this one neighbor who lived in a house on the side of him, and his name was Will H. He could sing his butt off. Will was only five years old at this time. Will and I, along with the other kids, would go to Mr. Jackson's house and sing, play, music, and dance. Mr. Jackson really enjoyed our company.

Will was like family to us. He would come over to our house every day to play with my little sister and me. Will sometimes would stay late and watch movies with my family. Whenever I went to Mr. Jackson's house, Will was right there singing with his golden voice.

In December of 1997, my aunt Belinda was having a Christmas program at her church.

They didn't have a drummer or any drums. At this time, I was still going to GMB Church. My aunt Belinda came up to me and asked me, "Can you play drums for our church Christmas program?" I told her yes. And the day of the program, I didn't just play drums—I played the bongos. My sister Brazil was right there by my side, and Will was singing in the program choir. After the program was over, the pastor, Reverend Victoria, came up to me and asked, "How would you like to play drums for the church every Sunday?" I was full of joy, and I said yes! That's when I started going to Ridge Chapel AME. I played on the bongos for about three months at Ridge.

One Sunday, I came to church, and Ridge had some drums. I didn't know what to do. I started playing drums, but I felt uncomfortable, so I went back to bongos. It took me a while to get used to the drums, but when I got used to the drums, I was unstoppable. I taped one of the drumsticks to my left arm when I played. At this time, my aunt Belinda; Ms. Gray, who was my aunt Belinda's mother; my cousins Starr and John; the pastor; and my aunt Belinda's family fell in love with me. I began a new family or, should I say, a second family.

It was awesome that God had opened doors for me that I never believed he could open. My life was really unfolding. Yet deep down inside, I was hurting and full of pain, but I didn't show it. There was still a little boy trapped in that prison mind crying to get out. I figured God had realized he had made a mistake, and that's why he allowed these good things to happen in my life.

I couldn't show my sister Brazil that I was unhappy and full of pain. She looked up to me. Truth be told, I was troubled. Everyone saw me as this strong person. It was like I was living a lie. That is one of the prison minds I formed: living a lie but trusting in God.

Do you live this lie at times? Do you pretend to be someone you're not? How many hearts are troubled today?

I have news for you:

> Do not let your hearts be troubled.
> Trust in God; trust also in me. (John
> 14:1)

Jesus is telling us he is the way to the Father. All you have to do is trust in him and trust in God the Father. But I didn't trust God. Instead of trusting God, I blamed him for all the negative things in my life over the years. I formed a lot of prisons in my mind, and there was no way of getting out.

CHAPTER 13

It's Time to Take a Stand

Life can be like a hurricane.
It has its storms, and it has its rain.
Life is a novel of unforgettable stories.
As life has its opportunities, we are
     pushed away day by day from our
     enemies.
They are taking what is not theirs, but
     who's to say that anyone cares?
As we walk through those open doors
     of pain, waiting patiently for that
     instant love to gain.
We feel hurt and lost in the woods, try-
     ing to do everything we could,
But we still feel disappointed and
     ashamed.
They say we are the ones to blame.
Now we want to disappear behind our
     tears and fears.

We try to hide aside the fake happiness,
  but deep down inside, we are full of
  loneliness.
Is there a way to discover what's gone,
  and why we feel so alone?
In our minds, we are saying, "Set us
  free by your might and rescue us
  through the night."
Today is the day, my friends, to put this
  madness to an end.
It's time to take a stand and say, "Yes, we
  can!"
Even if you fall, get back up, dust yourself off, and stand tall.
I know you are tired of being pushed
  around.
Now it's time for you to change that
  frown into a smile.
Life is what you make it to be whether it's
  happy, sad, mad, or mind free.
Let's take a stand and spread happiness, faithfulness, and peacefulness
  throughout the land.
I believe in you, and God does too.
It's time to take a stand!

Unfold Part 2

Since I've made so many friends in the sixth grade, I had reasons to talk on the phone. I talked on the phone so much it
was like I was addicted to it. My sister Kim was also addicted
to the phone. And since we only had one phone line, Kim
and I always fought over the phone. We would fight day and

night nonstop. Our father would have to tell us to stop fighting over the phone. Sometimes he will make us get off the phone and stay off for days.

Anger

Being the person I was in sixth grade after making so many friends, I started acting out.

Even though I had so many friends, I was still ashamed about my prosthetic leg. So when we had gym class, I never dressed out. Well, I remember that one day, I did something that could have hurt a lot of people. My anger took over me and formed a prison of its own.

All the other kids were dressing out for gym class. The gym teacher came up to me and said, "Why are you not dressing out?"

I looked at her and said, "Because I don't want to." I was very annoyed by her.

"Okay! You have not dressed out since you have been in this class. So if you don't dress out today, you will not be going outside with the rest of the class!" she said with a demanding tone.

So I sat down in the gym while the gym teacher took the rest of the class outside. As I was sitting, I was getting aggravated. I got up, and I started to leave the gym. Back then, when the teachers took attendance, they would put up their attendance sheets on their classroom doors for the attendance office to pick up.

Well, I started walking down the school halls picking up all the attendance sheets on the classroom doors. I headed back toward the gym. At Clear Junior High School, in the back of the gym, we had a washer and dryer. I started putting all the attendance sheets in the dryer. I was mad and angry at the gym teacher because she wouldn't let me go outside.

By the time I was about to start the dryer on one hundred degrees, the gym teacher came around the corner.

"What are you doing?" she yelled.

I was so shocked; I couldn't even move. The next thing that happened, I found myself in a whole lot of trouble. I was about to start a fire at my school because I couldn't get my way. I was mad at the teacher, and I blamed her. May anger took over me, and there was no turning back.

Do you let your anger get the best of you? Does your anger hold you captive? Do you blame people for making you angry? Do you say, "If he/she wouldn't have done it, I wouldn't be angry"?

We become so insensitive to our own sins that we don't notice we're the villain in our own lives. Anger is a powerful and natural emotion. Don't let it put you in that prison mind. The worst prison any man or woman can be confined in is the prison that they create within themselves. Remember:

> A fool gives full vent to his anger,
> but a wise man keeps himself under con-
> trol. (Proverbs 29:11)

*****

Tiffany and I were still dating in the seventh grade. I was in love with that girl. Tiffany brought out a different side of me that I didn't understand. I can't even explain it. I was still trapped in that prison mind, and pain rose every now and then. I soon realized that I was the center of attention. Not the attention that I was used to back in elementary school, but attention that makes a person popular.

In 1998, the doctors took away my prosthetic hand because I told them I could do more without it. My life was going so good, and I would have done anything to keep it that way. Yeah, okay, I did get a little big-headed. Hell, I was untouchable. So what can I say?

I thank Tiffany for bringing me out of my shell. I know I said I loved her dearly, but I did something to her, and even today she still doesn't know about it. Because I was so popular, the females at my school always hung around me. But who would have known that I would cheat on Tiffany after all she had done for me? My prison mind turned me into a monster. It led me to some type of drug that eased my pain.

Sex

The summer of 1998, there was this girl who lived in my neighborhood. One day she came over to my house, and we were sitting in the living room watching TV. One thing led to another, and I found myself not a virgin anymore. Not only had I cheated on Tiffany, but I felt different. What I mean is that it seems like all my pain, sorrow, depression, and all the other stuff that held me back just went away.

From that day on, my life really changed. I found something that I could use to cope with my pain. Sex was my drug. When I felt lonely, sad, or depressed, sex was my drug of choice. When I woke up in the mornings and examined myself, the mistake I believed that God had made my life, sex was there to ease my pain for the moment.

All kinds of people have their own ways of dealing with their pain, like alcohol and dope.

Sex was my painkiller. And for the girl that I had sex with, her life changed as well.

I didn't know how to deal with sex. I didn't really know anything about sex. I was never taught about sex. My parents never sat me down and talked to me about condoms, infections, or even having babies. I'm not saying that I was clueless about sex, but I figured if my parents didn't talk to me about sex, it wasn't important.

I finally found something that eased my pain, and there was no turning back. From the first time I had sex, I allowed my sexual desires to form into a prison mind that changed my life.

Not only did it change my life, but later down the line, it destroyed my life.

Many teens today are pressured into having sex. Their bodies are changing, and their hormones are going wild. Teens feel like they have to have sex to fit in. Teens also feel like sex is the right thing to do so they can feel more like a man or a woman. Listen! Sex can be dangerous outside of God's law.

Don't allow your sexual desires to form into a prison mind of lust. First Thessalonians 4:35 says,

> It is God's will that you should be
> sanctified: that you should avoid sexual
> immorality; that each of you should learn
> to control his own body in a way that is
> holy and honorable, not in passionate lust
> like the heathen, who do not know God.

After the first time I had sex, I couldn't control my own body. Satan now knew the weakness I had toward sex. And he used it for his own good.

Sexual desires may be placed under Christ's control. God created sex as an expression of love between a husband

and wife. Anything outside of that could be dangerous. Paul warns us not to let our lustful passions and thoughts control God's people. Flee from your sexual desires and remember your body is a temple of the Holy Spirit.

> Flee from sexual immorality. All other sins a man commits are outside of his body, but he who sins sexually sins against his own body. Do you not know that your body is a temple of the Holy Spirit, who is in you, whom you have received from God? You are not your own; you were bought at a price. Therefore, honor God with your body. (1 Corinthians 6:18–20)

Sex can bring diseases to our bodies. Sex outside of marriage violates you, and it can hurt others. Sex can affect our personalities and harm ourselves physically and spiritually.

Parents, please sit your teens down and talk to them about sex and how they should wait until they're married. Don't allow your child to form that prison mind of sexual desires through lustful ways or thoughts.

As a teen, I was a church person, and I believed in God. Being a Christian, we need to humble ourselves. At that time, I didn't know how to humble myself. I didn't believe I had the right path to follow in a situation such as sex. My parents had their own problems, and I guess they didn't feel the need to talk to me about sex. So the next time your sexual desires try to overtake you, pray and ask God to help you humble yourself.

Second Chronicles 7:14 says,

> If my people, who are called by
> my name, will humbles themselves and
> pray and seek my face and turn from
> their wicked ways, then I will hear from
> heaven and will forgive their sin and will
> heal their land.

Let me give you some tips on how God wants us to humble ourselves. First, admit your sins. Second, ask God for forgiveness, then seek God with all your heart. And finally, change your behavior. An idle mind is the devil's workshop. That means if you spend time doing nothing, you are giving Satan an open door to work on you. Start humbling yourselves to let God work in your life and not Satan.

CHAPTER 14

I discovered another gift that God had given me in the eighth grade. In 1999, I was in English class, and the teacher was teaching us how to write poetry. The first thing that came to my mind is "Poetry is for girls." Yes, I did write the so-called poetry, but I was just doing something so I could get an A. Well, my teacher, Mr. Webb, took a look at my poetry paper; and he was amazed. "Your poetry is amazing. I didn't know you could write poetry," Mr. Webb said cheerfully.

I paused for a second and said, "I didn't know I could write poetry either. I just thought of my girlfriend Tiffany, and I started writing."

I've been appreciating my own work ever since God gave me the gift to write poetry. I still remember the very first poem I wrote:

True Love

The sun comes shining through.
I see the beauty that's within you.
The moon and stars may fill the sky, but
    a smile from you will please my eye.

There's no need for me to pretend.
I hope our love will never end.
Can't you tell from the smile on my face
That you make this world a better place?

*****

My mind was trapped in all kinds of prisons, but that was okay because I learned how to control them—or so I thought. Around this time, Bank ISD was putting cameras in all the schools. At Clear Junior High school, I was the center of attention. The more I acted out, the more friend I gained.

One day, when they put cameras up in our school, a lot of my friends didn't believe that the cameras would be on. My friends and I thought they were putting fake cameras up to scare us. Because I wanted to be the center of attention, during the break between first and second period, I, being the fool that I was, stuck my penis out in front of one of the cameras. Everyone stopped and looked with an "I can't believe he did that" look.

Later that day, the principal came in and got me out of Mr. Webb's class. Sure enough, the cameras were real. I don't have to tell you what happened after that.

*****

Tiffany moved away February of 1999 with her mother to another state. I was really sad for her. Tiffany's parents filed for divorce. I was going to miss her. She was my joy, and Tiffany brought me out, and that's why I am who I am today. Also, I never got the chance to tell her I cheated on her with another female. When Tiffany left, I was really doing my own thing. Teachers called my parents and told them that if I didn't get my act together, I was going back to the eighth grade. At that time, I just didn't care.

I went to church every Sunday. I played the drums, and I praised God. Sad to say, my prison mind was still there. My prison mind wasn't free. God had opened so many doors for me, but I was fighting against him. That's what blinded me.

By the time March came around, my baby girl Suzanne was born. What a joy! The summer of 1999, my church Ridge Chapel was having a musical. So I walked down to Big Momma's house and asked my brother if he could help me do something for the program. He said yes. See, my brother can sing, rap, and do a lot of other things. About this time, my brother wasn't a Christian.

A few days before the musical, my brother came to me and said, "Josh, I want you to rap with me."

I looked at him like he was crazy. "I can't rap!"

My brother smiled. "I'll teach you."

So my brother wrote a rap that was called "If You Don't Know." The day of the program, my brother and I performed, and that was the day that I was put on the rap scene. I really enjoyed myself, and everyone loved me. My brother Ken made me a gospel rapper. I started writing my own raps, and my little sister Brazil started rapping with me.

Let me mention my brother for just a minute. My brother's son Mark was born July of 1999, and my brother also got married around that time. I believed my brother formed a prison mind toward our father. I really don't know what happened between my father and my brother before I was born. Whatever it was, that's why my brother was never really around my sisters and me. I can't really tell you if it was a form of prison mind, but it kept my brother away from us. And when my father and brother did come around each other, they would fight most of the time. I just didn't know why.

Don't get me wrong, my brother loves us. But whatever happened between him and my father, that's what stopped him from coming around. I can say this: when Mark was born, that brought my father and brother closer.

*****

I felt my heart drop to my feet when my parents filed for divorce in 1999. I didn't see that coming. I knew that they fought all the time. I just thought God would fix their problems, but he didn't. I was mad as hell at God. I felt like he failed me once again. The prison mind took over my parents and won.

"Two Become One" Was Broken

You ask, "Why?" It is because the Lord is acting as the witness between you and the wife of your youth, because you have broken faith with her, though she is your partner, the wife of your marriage covenant (Malachi 2:14). My parents broke the faith that they made with each other. Not only did they break their faith, but they broke the bond between each other that God had made.

The two become one:

> Has not the Lord God made them one? In flesh and spirit, they are his. And why one? Because he was seeking godly offspring. So, guard yourself in your spirit, and do not break faith with the wife of your youth. (Malachi 2:15)

My parents did not guard their spirit. So they allowed Satan to get into their heads. My parents did not just break their faith with each other, but they broke the spiritual purpose and relationship of being one with God.

> "I hate divorce," says the Lord God of Israel. "And I hate a man's covering himself with violence as well as with his garment," says the Lord Almighty. So, guard yourself in your spirit, and do not break faith. (Malachi 2:16)

"Do not break faith" means to have commitment to your spouse/marriage as God has commitment to his promises with his people.

When my parents filed for that divorce, I blamed God. I was so mad at him I said, "I'm going to do whatever I want. And because you made so many mistakes in my life, you are going to let me do what I want." How many of you know that is not how God works? I formed a prison mind that was very dangerous.

Later that year, I started to have dizzy spells. It was so bad to the point where I would have to go to the hospital at times. All this time there was a miracle sitting inside of me, waiting to come out for the world to see. But I was blinded. I formed a prison mind that wouldn't even let me see that miracle. God kept blessing me, and I didn't even know it was him. Please understand these words that you are reading, take the blindfold off your eyes, and see the same miracle-working God inside of you. People need to see miracles inside of you so they can believe. But first, you have to believe. Then you will discover all the miracles God has for you.

CHAPTER 15

A Letter to God

Dear God,

I'm writing you this letter because my life is really hard. I have been praying for the longest time, and I just don't know what to do. I have been told that if I turn to you, you will help me through. I'm tired of living this way and waking up trapped in my prison mind each and every day.

When I get on my knees to pray, I ask for wisdom, peace, faith, love, and understanding, for all of these attributes to be in me to stay. But I get no answer.

Why are you not answering me? Answer me! I know you are there because I can feel you in the cold midair. Can't you see my pain, my tears, and my fears in my heart? I don't know what the problem is. I've been worshiping you from the start.

But I still get no answer.

Answer me! Answer me! Please, God, answer me!

It seems like every time I pray, my prayers don't get no higher than the ceiling. I know you see me trying to get a spiritual healing. Are you mad at me? Are you disappointed with me?

Are you disgusted with me? What is it?

I already accepted your Son Jesus Christ as my Lord and Savior. There may be times I fell off with unpleasing behavior.

Can you hear me? I feel so alone. I can't make it on my own. Can you hear me? I'm hurting; I'm hurting deep down inside. I feel like you just pushed me to the side. I'm so lost and so confused. I feel so, so, so used. My body is shaking and my nerves racking. Can you hear my call? Why are you not answering, huh? Why? Why? Can you hear my cries?

I know I did things in my life I'm not glad about, and the things I've done I should have gotten caught. I already ask you to forgive me for those sins, but it still seems like you don't want to take me in. Is my life over? It feels like it's over. Father, just give me a sign to let me know my life is just going to be fine.

I'm screaming for you! I'm looking for you, and I'm reaching for you.

Your Word says, "You will never leave me; nor forsake me." Please don't let Satan take me. I know you won't put more on me than I can bear. At least I know you care. Someone once said, "God may not come when you want him, but he is always on time."

You're closer than I think, and I know you can be here faster than I can blink. I just need to be patient. I also pray for patience.

Thank you for understanding.

Love sincerely,
Joshua

Your Will vs. God's Will

The universe is going into a curse.
The world is sinking into all of their sins.
We say it's God's fault because we claim
    we've never been taught.
If you look at our situations and the world
    participations,
We're the ones who think we are powerful,
But it is God who is faithful.
As we express our true emotions, it's our
    actions that are guilty.
We don't want to take the responsibility
    to follow through what we need to
    do. It is a mental state
Of mind to all mankind that we made
    this earth for what it's worth.
God knows the plan that he made for all
    the land,
And if you think you are better than
    God, he can destroy every man.
Yes, we can kill and think we can heal,
But what is the point if we don't know
    the real deal?
Look at us taking prayers out of schools.
You think you did something?
You are dumb as fools.
We as people worship material things:
Silver, gold, and even diamond rings.
God can see clear through our troubles
    and fears.

God can wipe away every painful mem-
    ory and tear.
So, it is God's will, and he still holds the
    whole world in his hands.

Lost on the Road

Is it the lifestyle I live?
Or could it be the appearance that I give?
My mind is the one that is doing time.
It's difficult to face the everyday life
When people all around you are full of
    strife.
I'm closed in like four walls in a box.
Things are running through my mind
    constantly.
I try to focus and come back to reality.
I have so much frustration they all come
    at once.
Like a combination, the world calls it
    stress,
But I call it settling for less.
As I approach my stopping point and
    glance,
At the balance of where I stand
I can determine and transform myself
    into all I can be.
Now I understand the difference
Of this so-called "independence."
Stop depending on yourself and keep
    your eyes on God
Because if not, you will be lost on the
    road.

Walk on Water

Don't be afraid to take that step.
Keep the faith within yourself.
When the going gets tough and your life
    is really rough,
Keep your eyes on Christ's everlasting
    prize.
When you have strong storms in your life
    day by day.
Keep the faith because Christ will make
    you obey.
As the water gets high and darkness fills
    the sky,
Keep the faith because what Satan told
    you was all a lie.
When your money gets low and you
Have no place to go, don't be afraid
    because Jesus is your financial aid.
So, it's time to walk on water and stay
    focused on Christ,
Because He is the one who is guarding
    your life.
Walk on water and don't turn away,
Because if you do, your life is like a sheep
    that is astray.
When you feel yourself starting to sink
    and go under,
This is the point you need to start to
    wonder.
So, take the test and do your best.
So, when you pass on your soul can rest.

CHAPTER 16

Mistakes

When I was in high school, I was acting
 like a fool. I had girls over here,
And I had girls over there.
A part of me just didn't care.
I was making mistakes acting all fake.
My mother moved away, way out of town.
She left me alone to fight on this
 battleground.
I was mad at her,
And I didn't want to talk to her because
 she got remarried.
I thought she would start a new family
 without me.
This killed me mentally and emotionally.
As I got older, I started to look at life for
 what it was.
I started to realize what life can be about.
I wanted to help children in a tutoring
 program that failed,
In a neighborhood called Carverdale.

Changes

Carverdale became a neighborhood of drugs, hookers, cops, and killings in the year 2000.

I'm sure we always had them, but it had gotten worse over the past few years. Every time you turned around, someone got hurt or went to jail for selling drugs. Then some of the kids would go down to the corner store and buy cigarettes knowing they're underage. And by the time night fell, here came the hookers walking up and down the street trying to make a buck. Man, there went the neighborhood.

I pretty much looked the same. Of course, I got taller, and I was fourteen going on fifteen years old, and I was still slim.

The relationship with my mother wasn't good anymore. I wasn't even a mother's baby. I became a daddy's boy. I will live with my mother for a few months, then I will get mad at her, and then I will go live with my father. From time to time even though my parents were divorced, they would still find a way to fight.

My relationship with my siblings was pretty much the same as well. Kelly was the protector, Kim was the aggressor, Brazil was my best friend, and she loved me so much. As for Ken, he started coming around with my nephew Mark.

My little sister Brazil and I became very popular in the gospel rapping industry. Everyone loved us. We even came up with a group named TFC, which means "Teens for Christ." We'll go to church and rap to get the young people pumped up for God. That was our main focus, getting the young people more involved with God's business.

In the year 2000, my prison mind was still there. My prison mind wouldn't let go. My mind was sending me backward or, should I say, upside down. My problem was that I was trying to think like God, things like "I made a mistake on Josh, so he can do whatever he wants" or "Josh has been through too much, so I let him break my laws."

Isaiah 56:8 says,

> For my thoughts are not your thoughts, neither are your ways my ways.

That is what the Lord said. See, the people of Israel were crazy to think that they knew how God thinks or even acted like they knew his plans. God's knowledge is greater than man's knowledge. So stop trying to fit God into your plans to make it comfortable for you.

That's all I was trying to do, fit God in how I wanted him so I can feel better about myself. But truth be told, we need to strive to fit into God's plan and not our own.

What I learn throughout my life was to live, you must die.

> For whoever wants to save his life will lose it, but whoever loses his life for me, and the gospel will save it. (Mark 8:35)

To gain, you must give. Jesus said,

> If you want to be perfect, go, sell your possessions, and give to the poor, and you will have treasures in heaven. Then come, follow me. (Matthew 19:21)

Blessed are those who mourn. Matthew 5:4 says,

> Blessed are those who mourn, for they will be comforted.

To rule, you must serve. Luke 22:26 says,

> But you are not to be like that. Instead, the greater among you should be like the youngest, and the one who rule like the one who serves.

Suffering has a purpose. First Peter 5:10 says,

> And the God of all grace, who called you to his eternal glory in Christ, after you have suffered a little while, will himself restore you and make you strong, firm and steadfast.

As a teenage boy, I was selfish. I was worried about saving my life and not others. I was trying to gain, not give. Yes, I was rapping, but it was because I liked the fame. When I mourn, it was because I wanted God to feel sorry for me. I didn't really want to serve; I just wanted to be popular. And I was suffering because my prison mind had me thinking I can do whatever I wanted. I am here to tell you, do not let Satan hold you captive. I opened the door for Satan to come in, and at this time in my life, I couldn't find the door to let him out. So when you think or feel like you're upside down, just get on your knees and ask God to turn you right side up.

Since my parents had been divorced, my mother had found herself a boyfriend. His name was David G. I didn't like him much. I'm sure he was with my mother because she was beautiful. My mother was tall and had smooth brown skin and pretty smile. She kept her hair always short, and she had amazing eyes. She was just downright gorgeous. My father had a girlfriend as well. I can't remember her name because my father really never brought her around the house. I'm sure she was with my father because he was a very handsome man. My father was short, not fat, but a little round; he kept a low-cut hairstyle, and he dressed really nice.

I made a lot of mistakes in my life. And all I can say is learn from your mistakes. When you feel yourself about to fall, allow God to pick you back up.

CHAPTER 17

After I'd gotten myself into trouble all through junior high school, I finally made it to high school. Back when I was in eighth grade, one of my teachers called my father and told him, "If Josh doesn't straighten up his act, he will fail. Josh won't be able to go to the ninth grade." So my father got me straight. When I was in the ninth grade, I went to Fanta High School in Banks ISD in the year 2000.

The moment I entered into Fanta High School, it was easy for me to make friends. My life was going very good at this time. I was one of the most popular teens in school. And it wasn't because of football or any other sports. The young ladies loved me because I was a gospel rapper, I wrote poetry, I played the drums, and I was a unique young man. The other teens liked hanging around me because I had the females, and I was still acting out.

In the ninth grade, I had girlfriends after girlfriends. I didn't care I was acting wild. A part of me was still hurting deep down inside. I didn't go on a lot of dates, just a few. Dating was not on my mind. I just wanted to have sex.

So I had sex with all types of females. I couldn't control myself. I would sneak females into my house when every-one was asleep. I would take them into my room and have sex with them. My prison mind was controlling me. I didn't use condoms when having sex or even cared about AIDS or

STDs. It wasn't on my mind that I could kill her or she could kill me with a sexually transmitted disease.

There was just a part of me that didn't give a damn. Sex was my drugs, and I needed it more. I had a problem, and I didn't have help to fix that problem.

Jasper and I had been best friends since grade school. Truth be told, he was my only true best friend other than my little sister Brazil. Jasper wasn't hanging around me because I had females, and I was acting out. He'd been by my side when I was a nobody. Jasper wasn't a troublemaker. As a matter of fact, I don't think he ever got into trouble; at least I didn't see him get into any trouble.

Jasper was quiet; he was an observer. He paid attention to everything and everyone. If you asked me, I believed he was picky (picky toward the young ladies). Jasper was careful, and that's the good thing about him. Unlike me, who just jumped out there not thinking about the trouble I could get into.

Discipline

When I got to high school, I was really acting like a fool, doing things I wasn't supposed to do. Dating different girls every month. It was like I didn't care about anything or anyone. My father had to discipline me all the time. I was out of control.

Do you hate discipline? I know I did. Every time my father disciplined me, I got mad, got upset, and acted out more. But understand this, discipline is good. Now I know you think I'm crazy, but the Bible says,

> Whoever loves discipline loves knowledge, but he who hates correction is stupid. (Proverbs 12:1)

I hated correction, but God put discipline on this earth so we can learn from our mistakes and learn from the wisdom of others. When I was a teenager, I had a problem with my pride. I couldn't take constructive criticism. If someone tried to tell me something, I would curse them out.

Revelation 4:19 says,

> Those whom I love I rebuke and discipline. So be earnest, and repent.

If God didn't love us, he wouldn't discipline us. I had to learn the hard way. I was lying to myself. God didn't put discipline on this earth to punish us, but he put discipline on earth to bring us closer to him. We can avoid God's discipline by staying closer to him through confession, service, worship, and studying God's Word. So don't give up on God when things aren't going your way. When you feel like you're being disciplined, just look at it like God is saying, "My child, come back to me."

Have you ever lived a double life? What I mean is that with one group of people you act one way, and with another group of people you are a different person. You pretend to be somebody you're not. When I entered into my teenage years, I was living a double life. When I was at school, I acted like a fool and had sex with all different types of girls, but when I was at church or at home or somewhere else, I acted like a perfect angel.

Being Strong

A lot of people thought I was a strong-minded person, but if you take the makeup off me, I was weak. When I thought about all the pain I went through as a child, and when I looked at myself in the mirror, I didn't see a strong person. I saw a weak, powerless Christian who let the devil run all over him. In my own sight, I saw myself as a grasshopper just like the Israelites. You see, the Israelites were scared to fight the giants. It wasn't because the giants were too big, but the Israelites saw themselves as small and not strong. So in their own sight, they saw themselves as grasshoppers, and that's what defeated them.

As a true believer in Christ, stop seeing yourself as small and weak like the Israelites. Look at yourself as a conqueror in the strength of God Almighty. And if you're not a believer, seek and you shall find. The devil would rather not be around a believer in Christ who is strong and bold.

Being a teenager, I was in church, and I was a believer, but I didn't see myself as strong and powerful. I can truly say I let the devil play with my mind. No one knew my true identity because I lived that double life.

If you are not strong and powerful in God, it's time to change that. It's time to be full of God's Word and Holy Ghost. It's time for you to start walking around like God's spiritual giants and change the devil into that small grasshopper. Are you a warrior? Or are you Satan's wimp?

Now you decide.

To read more about the Israelites and the giants, you can find it in Numbers 13:17–33.

CHAPTER 18

Sexual Evolution

Sex,
Something that feels so good.
Sex,
Something we dream of wishing that it
     would.
Sex,
The passion that brings us through.
Sex,
Just to think that she's riding on top of
     you.
Wait!
Stop!
Let's take this back to the top.
Young man, trying to do everything you
     can.
You're driving around
Picking up every girl in town.
Thinking you are a playa,
But you are really a sexual hatta.
You're taking the ladies back to your
     place
Getting them in the mood,
Making them feel good

Inside with a smile on their faces.
You're doing everything to make them
    feel low, down, and dirty
And they are liking it.
She was looking all good:
5'5", brown eyes, and thick between the
    thighs.
You know you were going to hit that as
    you were beating her cat.
Not knowing that so-called "making of
    the love"
Without using a glove
Will bring you down a path of hurt,
Blinded, and not being alert.
You thought she easy,
But her sex was really cheesy.
Now you caught a disease called STD.
So sad,
Now you are mad.
Young lady,
Your life is really shady.
You know you look good
Doing everything you could.
Trying to find the right one
But doing it wrong
By sleeping with the fathers and their
    sons.
You think sex is a game,
But deep down inside you feel so
    ashamed.
Every week it's another bed:
Josh, John, Eric, and Ted.
You want the right guy,

But you know they're all a lie.
You are having babies here and there,
But to those children life isn't fair.
You are the type of female that likes to
     get hit from the back,
And when the guys are inside of your
     body you don't know how to act.
You have a name that's going around
     town.
They call you the "City Hoe"
Because you are always on the go.
Your legs open wide
Behind closed doors trying to hide.
Not using your brain,
You're going insane
Because you now have AIDS,
Your life is about to fade.
Watching your family cry
Because you are about to die.
You're praying to God asking him,
"Why?"
Looking back on what you've done in
     your mind you thought it was fun.
Your kids don't know what's going on.
All they know is "momma sick,"
And they feel all alone.
Well, this is it
Your life is about to quit.
Now she's dead at the age of nineteen,
And there is a lot in this world she hasn't
     seen.

Listen, rap it up! Get tested!

Dealing with Sex

Now it's 2001, and sex was a part of my life. I allowed sex to take over me. Sex was all I can think about. My drug, my love for sex, was all I wanted. All this time I was stuck in the past, and so I used sex as a crutch. Even though my life was going good right now and everyone loved me, I still thought about the pain that I trapped into my heart. Sex for me was the other half of me.

Sex polluted my mind to the point where I started having sex with my cousins. I knew it was wrong, and they knew it too, but that's just the way it was. Sex was my high. Have you ever gotten so high it made you feel so damn good for the moment? I did with sex. Playing the drums was my high at first, but for some reason, it wasn't getting me high anymore. Maybe because people were praising me for playing the drums. So I turned to sex. You know, it's like drinking alcohol, and for whatever reason, it's not making you feel good anymore, so you turned to popping pills or shooting up dope. That was me turning to another high.

Sex can be like venom flowing through your veins, poisoning your mind to where there's no end. Sex is not a game, and it can hurt you. It can destroy you.

> Food for the stomach and the stomach for food but God will destroy them both. The body is not meant for sexual immorality, but for the Lord, and the Lord for the body. (1 Corinthians 6:13)

Freedom, God gave that to us. Free from sin and free from Satan. We are free to enjoy everything that comes from God. We shouldn't abuse that freedom, which most of us do.

God wants us to enjoy sex through marriage. We have to be careful so that what God allows us to enjoy won't turn into a bad habit that can control us. I allowed sex to take over my mind. Sex is a temptation that is in our everyday lives. Don't ever underestimate the power of sex. Satan can use sex to take over your soul. God is our protector so we won't destroy ourselves or destroy others. When we feel loneliness, desires, and depressed, God will fill us with himself.

By the time I got to the tenth grade, I was out of control. I was getting into too much trouble. In school, I would get detention just about every day. At home, my father would punish me all the time. It seems like there was no end. At first, getting into trouble was fun, but it became a part of my life.

It was the middle of my tenth-grade year when this amazing thing happened to me. Someone who believed in me gave me a chance and changed my life. This man put something in me I didn't know I had. Mr. Jerry R. was the associate principal at Fanta High School. He took the time to work with me. And that's when I realized I wanted to make a difference. I wanted to help children who were going through the same problems I was going through. Mr. Jerry gave me a job.

I started working at Fanta High School answering phones. Also, I started working after school tutoring little kids at the Carverdale Reading Program in Banks ISD. I really enjoyed working, making a difference. I started being good in school and making good grades. I lost half of my so-called friends. Thank God Jasper was still by my side.

At my church, I became a youth president. Things really started to look up for me. Making a difference was cool, and I enjoyed it. Later that year, I met this family that moved to my neighborhood. They lived right down the street from my house. They were DeDe and her twin brothers, Luck and Larry. DeDe was about two years younger than, me and Luck and Larry were about eight years old. And their mother was a very sweet lady. Ms. Stacy was her name.

One day I was walking down the street, and I heard the twins rapping. So I stopped at their house, and I listened. After they finished rapping, I told them they were pretty good. I explained to them about the gospel group my sister and I were in. I asked the twins if they wanted to be a part of the group. They said yes. The twins had really never been to church, so it was a learning thing for them.

Teens for Christ, our group, became a known rapping gospel group. It was me, my little sister Brazil, the twins, Will from across the street, and Mary. Mary was my brother's cousin from his mother's side of the family. DeDe and I became best friends. And I became a big brother to the twins. We all were like one big happy family.

CHAPTER 19

It's not every day that your life changes from bad to good and from good to worse. By the end of my tenth-grade year, my life began to change. Some people may think that change is good. But to me, that change went from bad to good and from good to worse. I was pretending to be someone I'm not. And it was killing me deep down inside.

I knew I was trapped in my own mind. My pain would come and go, and when the pain came, I had sex to get rid of it. But no one knew how I felt because I always kept a smile on my face. Even though I was this popular teenager, I felt so alone. I couldn't talk to anyone to tell them how I felt because I didn't want to let them down. People believed I was this strong person and nothing could break me.

About this time, I believed I was broken, and glue couldn't even fix me. I was unhappy, and I was troubled. My life was miserable, and the bad part about it was I was the only one who noticed my problems. How can I help others if I was discouraged myself? That really bothered me, but I couldn't back down now. So I was living this lie, and I convinced myself it was okay. What I learned throughout my life was that you can be bruised but not broken. You can fall time after time, but you can get back up again. That's the beauty of my God. He won't allow Satan to break you or make you. All you have to do is just believe and have faith and stop pretending. In June of 2002, Mr. Jerry signed me up at this camp called New Day Camp. This camp was designed for disabled children to go and just have fun. This camp taught us how to learn to accept who we are. I had fun, and it was a great experience. The counselors were awesome. They helped us a lot. But I just couldn't accept who I was. So that's what made it hard for me.

In July or August of 2002, I played this game that gave me a new look on life down the line. This game is what made me realize I was messing up. Even though it wasn't as bad as people made it to be, it was still wrong.

I was seventeen years old, and I should have known better. One day Will, the twins, and I were at my home; and we had nothing to do. Well, we decided to play truth or dare. We didn't make anyone do nasty stuff, but we dared Will to run around the house butt naked, so he did. The twins and I turned our heads, and we didn't even look. Now that I thought about it, I shouldn't have played that game with nine-year-olds. Truth or dare is just not a good game to play.

Most people would think my little sister looked up to me; maybe she did. But the funny and crazy thing was I'm the one who looked up to my little sister Brazil. Why? Because she was smart and beautiful. And our family would always say good things about her. Truth be told, I was jealous of Brazil. I felt like she was perfect.

What made me feel so good was the kids at the Carverdale Reading Program. They all looked up to me. Every day after school I looked forward to going to work at the Reading Program. The kids there always put a smile on my face. If only I could have gotten rid of my prison mind, I would have been okay. The children at the Reading Program made me feel special. That's why I couldn't show them my true self. I didn't want to disappoint them.

When I entered into the eleventh grade, from what people were seeing in me, my life was good. I thought I was doing something right because the dizzy spells that I had were gone. I wasn't really in special ed anymore. And the computer Ms. Lockheart and her family gave me was taken away because my writing had improved. So if all these things that were supposed to be right were happening to me, why did I still feel trapped?

My family always had get-togethers and Sunday dinners. We did things like that. I hated going to the family gatherings because when I did go, they always talked good about Brazil, Starr, and John. Also, they talked about how cute Kim was and how pretty Kelly was. They never said anything good about me. I mean, they didn't say anything bad either, but I felt left out. I was doing good, helping kids, playing the drums, gospel rapping, and writing poetry. No one in the family talked about my good deeds. So I hated going to those family gatherings.

There's one thing I forgot to mention. At the age of fifteen, I got my driver's license. It's a funny story—well, at the time it wasn't so funny. My father went out of town, and he left his car and his car keys. I figured my father would never find out if I took his car for a spin. After I took the car for a few hours, I was driving back to the house. As I turned on our street, I saw my sister Kelly's car parked in the driveway. Crazy that I was, I left the car down the street.

By the time I walked back to the house, Kelly was standing outside. She asked, "Where is Daddy's car?"

"I don't know," I replied worriedly. "I guess he decided to take it with him."

But for some reason, Kelly looked down the street and said, "That looks like Daddy's car down there." She pointed toward the car. Then she looked at me funny.

"Okay, I admit I took Daddy's car for a spin." I was scared out of my mind.

Kelly was quiet for a few minutes, and then she said with a smile on her face, "I'm not going to tell on you. But you have to do whatever I tell you to do. If not, I will tell Daddy you took his car." She had an evil grin on her face.

To make a long story short, my daddy came back, and I was being blackmailed by my elder sister Kelly.

About a month later, I got tired of Kelly blackmailing me, so Kelly decided to tell on me, when I stopped doing what she wanted me to do. My father was mad at first, but he told me he was going to put me in driver's ed. That's how I got my driver's license. I thought I was going to get a beatdown, but instead, I went to driving school so I can drive legally.

I know some of you are asking, "Why does Kelly have a different last name than the rest of us?" You know, at one point Kelly's last name was R. Then she changed it to M. A while back when our mother told Kelly my father was not her father, she changed her last name to our mother's last name. I can't really imagine how Kelly felt, but if it was me, I would have melted. Later down the line, Kelly did find out who her father really was, but he still wasn't in her life as much.

Did Kelly create a prison mind for herself? She probably did. From my understanding, since she found out my father wasn't her father, she felt like my father's side of the family treated her different. Kelly thought she was an outcast.

My father loved Kelly like she was his own. Kelly loved my father. Even today, she still calls him Daddy. And my dad still calls Kelly his child. My brother Ken also loves my sister and would do anything for her just like the rest of us. And by the way, Kelly had a beautiful baby boy in January of 2001. His name is Toney J. Everyone says he looks just like me. Even today people say the same thing. Now I have two beautiful nephews.

Being Lost

It was now the end of 2002, and a lot had happened. I never did feel good about myself. As a matter of fact, I was lost. My mind, soul, and body were lost. I really didn't know who I was. It was like I was having an identity crisis. I was living this lie that made me who I was.

I needed to be saved. Hell, I thought I was saved because I was going to church, playing the drums, rapping gospel, and helping others. I was blinded by my prison mind. Sex overpowered me. I was lost, and no one could save me even if they tried. I needed to come back to Jesus.

If you read in Luke 15:1–7, Jesus was telling the Pharisees a parable about the lost sheep. Jesus was teaching that if you had a hundred sheep and you lost one, wouldn't you go and leave your ninety-nine sheep behind to find that one? And as you read on in Luke 15:1–7, it says when you find that one, you will joyfully put it on your shoulder and take it home.

By the time you get home, you'll call everyone you know and tell them to rejoice with you because you found your lost sheep. Just like Jesus said, "It's the same way in heaven, if one sinner repents than over the ninety-nine righteous people who do not need to repent, heaven rejoices." I didn't know what repentance was, or I just didn't care. All the sins I'd done were about to lead me down a path I didn't want to go.

You may think it was foolish for the shepherd to leave the rest of his sheep behind to find one. The shepherd knew all the other sheep would be fine, but that one was in danger. I was in danger, and I just didn't know it. God was searching for me, but I was refusing his rescue.

All the sheep were of high value, and the shepherd knew if he finds that one, it would be worth it. God's love is so great he seeks each individual out and rejoices when he finds them.

God gives us his mercy, and before we become believers, God searches us out, and he is still searching for those who are lost today. And if you're not a believer, please seek God because you don't want to be in the prison mind, and you don't want to be lost forever. Seek that freedom because it's there; you just have to find it. Remember it's the man who makes the mistake, not the mistake who makes the man.

✿

CHAPTER 20

I believe my sister Kim had a prison mind of her own. As I remember, Kim was always mean and evil. She tried to flush my head down the toilet. I don't know how, and I don't know when, but Kim created this evilness in her head a long time ago.

I remember a time when Kim chased my other sister Kelly around the house with a knife. For some reason, she created that darkness, and she used it to her own advantage. If my memory serves me right, Kim was mean to everyone. That was who she was. Kim in some cases was a loner. Also, I believe Kim was boy crazy. That's what made her a sex addict too.

There would be times my parents would have to leave us at the house to go find Kim. And of course, they would find her with some boy. Why was Kim the way she was? She wasn't just mean to my sisters and me, but she would fight anyone who she thought would get in her way.

In 2003, my mother was already married to David G., and they had moved out of Houston. I was mad at my mother. She moved out of town, and I thought she would forget about me. I was so mad at my mother because I thought she was going to start a new family. And at times when my mother called my father's house, she would ask to speak to my sisters instead of me. Sometimes when I spoke with my mother on the phone, she wouldn't talk to me long, but she would converse with my sisters for a long time.

I felt like my mother left me here to fight on this battleground all by myself. Don't get me wrong, my mother is a good mother. How many of you know that you're not alone? The battle is not yours; it's the Lord's. No matter what you are going through, let the Lord fight your battles for you.

> Do not be afraid of them; the Lord
> your God himself will fight for you.
> (Deuteronomy 3:22)

This scripture is talking about Joshua when he was leading his men to fight against the evil in the promised land. God promised Joshua that he would help him win every battle, so Joshua had nothing to fear. The promise remains the same for us today. Whether you are trying to fight temptation or trying to fight the battle of your prison mind, God promised to fight with us and for us. All you have to do is put your faith, hope, and confidence in him.

When my mother had moved away, I got closer to my aunt Belinda's side of the family. Even though my aunt Belinda's side of the family was no kin to me, I became a part of her family. The crazy part of this situation was that I always went to their family gatherings more than my family gatherings. You see, I was a selfish young man. I wanted everything to be about me.

I hung around my aunt Belinda's side of the family because they always talked good about me. My family I believe would always talk good about the rest of the children on my daddy's side of the family. My aunt Belinda's side of the family made me feel comfortable. I loved being part of her family. They were always there for me. My aunt Belinda was like my second mother. She'd been there for me through it all.

For some reason, I just couldn't talk to my aunt Belinda to tell her how I really felt. My aunt Belinda's side of the family believed I was this strong person, but I guess I fooled them.

Since my mother moved away, I just didn't care anymore. So now at this time I was just doing what I wanted to do. I didn't want people to feel sorry for me because I felt sorry for myself. Now I was really blaming God. I realized my mother had a life too. I was selfish, and I wanted life to be all about me.

When my mother would come drive to Houston to visit us sometimes, she and my father would fight. I would be on my father's side, and my sisters would be on my mother's side. Is that normal? I don't think we knew what the hell we were doing. We would just pick sides every time my parents fought.

I felt like God owed me. So I really got out there by having sex and more sex without using condoms. I didn't think God would punish me. I believed at times that he knew he made a mistake and brought me through hell to let me do what I wanted. How many of you know that God doesn't work like that?

One day a girlfriend came over to my house, and we had unprotected sex. A few days later, I was at work at the Reading Program, and I started walking down the hallway when I felt this pain in between my legs. I fell to my knees, and I lay down on the floor. One of the teachers saw me and rushed over to where I was lying. She asked me if I was okay, and I told her no. The next thing I knew, I was on my way to the hospital. My father met us there.

The girl I was having sex with at the time gave me an STD. One of the nurses gave me a shot in my butt. The nurse told me she wasn't going to tell my father, but I needed to be more careful next time. Did I listen? Did it stop me from having sex unprotected? In the beginning of 2003 was the first time I got an STD.

My prison mind blocked the side effects that my high was giving me. One of the side effects the drug of sex can give you is an STD. Even though I got an STD, I still was having sex with different females unprotected. What the hell was wrong with me? I just didn't care, I guess.

I was still jealous of my little sister Brazil. I really don't know why. There was something about her that made me feel the way I did. Maybe because I was looking at what God blessed her with instead of what God has done for me. Brazil was smarter than I, she was beautiful, and I felt like the family liked her better. "What has God done for me lately?" was my question.

> Don't I have the right to do what I want with my own money? Or are you envious because I am generous? So, the last will be first, and the first will be last. (Matthew 20:15–16)

Have you ever been jealous of what God has done or given someone else? If so, instead of being jealous of that person, focus on what God has blessed you with. Also, thank him for what he's done in your life. As a young man, I didn't understand that. God has done a lot for me. If I had seen that then as I see it now, I could have been free—free from the pain, because I know God would take care of me if I let go and let God!

I loved gospel rapping. I was glad when I included the twins Luck and Larry, Mary, Will, and Brazil to the gospel group. It was amazing to see the young ladies falling in love with the twins. So I decided to change the group name from Teens for Christ to the Gospel Twinz. The twins were the "show."

Since I changed the group name to the Gospel Twinz, we were doing more shows. There were times where we would go to churches after churches. Sometimes we performed at my church Ridge Chapel. Around this time, my little sister Brazil and I backed up from rapping and became the managers of the Gospel Twinz. The spotlight was on the twins. Don't get me wrong, everyone loved Will and Mary as well, but the twins were more popular.

Most of the time when we practiced, Will would be lazy. He didn't want to practice at all. Then Will would start confusion with the rest of the group. Sometimes it would be a big mess.

Peace

In 2003, I felt like I was missing something. Good things were happening to me, and I felt like I was drained and unaccepted. I was without peace. I didn't have peace within myself. I didn't accept myself for who I was. I lived on my past, and because of it, my past was controlling me.

I needed to find peace.

> Therefore, since we have been justified through faith, we have peace with God through our Lord Jesus Christ. (Romans 5:1)

I believe in Christ, but I didn't have the faith or peace that God was talking about. We have to understand that our acceptance with God is secure. We are complete through the Son of God.

And yes, we are going to face temptations, and we will have problems. But the problems we face daily will often help us grow. I wish I had understood that when I was entering into adulthood. Maybe I would have had peace.

> Let the peace of Christ rule in your hearts, since as members of one body you were called to peace. And be thankful. (Colossians 3:15)

That was my problem—I wasn't letting Christ rule over my heart. We need to understand that Paul is letting us know to let Jesus's peace conduct and rule in our hearts. Our feelings and desires clash. How can we deal with these conflicts and live by God's Word?

> Whatever you have learned or received or heard from me or seen in me—put it into practice. And the God of peace will be with you. (Philippians 4:9)

May of 2003 was my prom. Man, I was looking good! I was wearing a white suit with a nice undershirt with it. I had on nice black church shoes I called them. I was wearing an earring in my left ear that my mom bought me for my sixteenth birthday. And my hair was low cut. My date was looking good as well. She was wearing this hot, sexy red tight dress. Her body was out of this world. She had long hair, and her shoes were red pumps. We were bad (Michael Jackson bad).

When my date and I got to the prom, something went wrong. It came back. My dizzy spells came back. I got so sick I had to go lie down. So we left the prom early, but we didn't let it mess up our night. I went home and lay down until 1:00 a.m. Then my date and I went back out.

June 2003, I finally made it. I graduated from Fanta High School with a smile on my face. I walked across that stage holding my diploma in my hand. What a joy it was. Now it's time to move on to the next step in my life.

I was ready to leave home. Now that I was out of school, I had been playing the drums with Brother Kyle G. Brother Kyle was my aunt Belinda's brother. Brother Kyle G. and I would go to different churches that had musicals, and we would play music together. Brother Kyle G. played the bass guitar, and we were "Michael Jackson bad." Brother Kyle G. and I were like a small band. We had fun going to different churches. Brother Kyle G. also played the bass guitar at Ridge Chapel AME Church.

The summer of 2003, I went back to New Day Camp for the last time as a camper. Once again, I had fun, but I wasn't willing to learn. My prison mind blocked me from learning about the real me.

December of 2003, Kelly had another beautiful baby boy named Matthew J. It was time for me to get serious, but my prison mind was winning over me. I still was having sex. I still was doing what I wanted to do. And I still was living this lie and hiding behind a fake smile. Little did I know, I was crying for God to help me.

> O God, you are my God, earnestly I
> seek you; my soul thirsts for you, in a dry

and weary land where there is no water...
On my bed I remember you; I think of
you through the watches of the night.
(Psalm 63:1, 6)

CHAPTER 21

Identity Crisis

My name is Larry G. I've been asked by the author to tell you about myself. It is difficult because at one point in my life, I became another person.

At the age of nineteen, I received a fifty-year sentence for intoxicated manslaughter and aggravated assault with a deadly weapon. I have been locked up for twenty-three years. During that period of my life, many things changed.

First and foremost, August 16, 2011, my mother, brother, and sister were killed by a drunk driver. My mother was someone I loved more than anything and anyone. I killed some people from my carelessness of drinking and driving. Someone I loved was also killed that way. To this day, I'm angry and filled with hatred. At times I feel as though God has betrayed me.

At times I'm also angry because I don't know my true self. It's funny, but I have what they call "monkey" mind. My thoughts jump all over the place. And it is very difficult for me to get to a point where the world goes away and I can find myself the truth of my being, but I will keep working on it.

Someone once told me that sometimes it takes several lifetimes to find out what you are here for. I have asked the author, "What should I do if I meet the person who killed my mother, brother, and sister?" I have worked hard at forgiving that person. Sometimes I think I have, but deep in my soul there might yet remain a sliver of hatred. I worry about what might happen if I ever did see him. Such a meeting. This would be a severe test of my emotional and somewhat spiritual progress.

Author's Note: Larry was going through things in his life. He allowed drinking to take over him to the point where he killed someone. Not only did he kill someone, but he shot a man because the man was trying to stop him from fleeing the scene.

Through Larry's carelessness, God has turned the tables on him. Now Larry has to suffer the loss of his mother, brother, and sister. So Larry believes God has betrayed him. But truth be told, God is teaching him a lifelong lesson.

Larry took away someone's life by driving drunk. Another person took away Larry's mother's, sister's, and brother's lives. Do you see what's going on? Then Larry said he felt hatred toward the man who killed his family.

Do you think the family of the person Larry killed hates him? I believe Larry needs to learn how to forgive, and then he can be forgiven by his victim's family. God already forgave Larry; now Larry needs to forgive himself. Larry has to face up to God and ask him to give himself that same forgiveness.

As Fresh As April Roses

Rain comes falling from sweet heavenly
    skies.
Dropping holy water faithfully into every
    one's eyes.
Joy comes in the morning with a smile of
    a special blessing here and there

That God has repaired throughout each
  holy year.
Only this joy can come falling from
  heavenly skies.
As fresh as April Roses will tell no lies.
Enjoy the smell of the spring as white
  doves fly in the sky,
As they sing,
"Holy, Holy, Holy, how great is his glory."
As fresh as this world can be.
As April Roses rise from the ground and
  open around heavenly trees.
The heavens open up
Pouring out a blessing overflowing your
  cup.
The pain has gone away
And the love for Christ will remain and
  stay.
As fresh as April Roses as they will be.
As fresh as April Roses I hope that you'll
  see.
As fresh as April Roses,
As fresh as April Roses,
As fresh as April Roses,
This is life's main key.
Stay away
And don't come back!

I've let you take over my life way too long.
You even been in places where you don't
  belong.
You tried to make me believe things that
  weren't true,

But I was a fool because I don't belong
    to you.
You tried to put a cover over my eyes so
    that I couldn't see all the lies.
You wanted me to believe in you, to fol-
    low you, and to turn away from
The ONE who died on the cross for my
    sins.
You wanted me to be like you, lost, and to
    believe that the Scriptures are false.
There's an ongoing battle between evil
    and good.
I have fought harder than I thought I
    would.
But you know my weakness in times that
    I fall.
You tried to cover up my mouth so God
    couldn't hear my calls.
As I pray, you make me feel like the Lord
    isn't there.
I feel ashamed like life isn't fair.
See, I have to be careful and look behind
    my back,
Because you will creep in and try to
    attack.
You be tempting me to do things I don't
    mean.
You don't care for anyone, not even your-
    self, or God's only Son.
Well today is the day that I will make a
    stand to say,

"Stay away and don't come back because
    this child of God is cleaning up his
    act!"
Peace!

I'll Rise

The world is getting bad and if you look
    at it, it's really sad.
We're living in our last days, so wake up
    and come out of that faze.
Our greatest weakness may be our failure
    to rely on God's strength.
The season will come, and the season
    will go.
Through it all your heart may never
    know.
We as people are living with past scars.
It's okay to feel pain.
Sometimes it's okay to feel alone.
Now it's time to reach for the stars.
Life and peace, it's okay to live again,
But forgive yourself for whatever you did
    back then.
Leave it there and let Christ take care of
    its fair.
Conflict of the spirit with flesh some-
    thing we all go through like a sugar
    rush.
No one has control of their own destiny
    but God himself.
It's up to you to live up to your
    responsibilities.

If you don't make plans for tomorrow,
How are we going to make it through
today?
All hope isn't lost, but soon hope will
find its way.
Fight the giants in your life,
And take back the victory you won,
Because no pain is forever.
Speaking from the mind, we all do in
time.
All of us live in some type of prison
No matter if it's physically, mentally, or
emotionally.
Most of the time it can be sexually, but
we lived.
We live in that prison of weakness,
We live in that prison of doubtfulness,
We live in that prison of lack of
self-control,
And we live in that prison for our ene-
mies to grab a hold.
But now is the time to say I'll rise!
I'll rise higher than a mountain.
I'll rise clear like water from a drinking
fountain.
I'll rise beyond the sun.
I'll rise through the park as the kids are
having fun.
I'll rise just as a beautiful butterfly.
I'll rise beyond the birds in the sky.
I'll rise when my enemies tried to bring
me down.

I'll rise with a smile on my face instead
    of a frown.
I'll rise when I walked across the stage
    holding my diploma.
I'll rise when I get sick and all I had was
    a cold instead of falling into a coma.
I'll rise bigger than a stereo system, but
    all the world wants to do is just
    twist them.
I'll rise when I came to prison,
And I will rise when I leave prison,
But through it all I will RISE
And so can you!

CHAPTER 22

Lost

At last! I graduated with a smile on my face.
I could have not done it without Jesus
    Christ and the blood of his grace.
When I left high school, I really thought
    I was cool,
Still living in sin doing all I can.
I had a gospel rap group with two teen-
    age boys that are twins.
I wanted to do right by God so I can give
    them a helping hand.
Life was great!
I've motivated kids,
I had my own place,
My own car,
And my own money.
I had a great pastor along with a praying
    church family.
But I still fell short of the glory of God.
I was still lying up with girls
Thinking they were my world.
All this time I was lost, not knowing that
    someday
I will have to pay the cost.

Loss vs. Freedom

In 2004, Carverdale was the same—the drugs, the hookers, the cops, and so on. The kids were always fighting each other after they got off the school bus. Cops were always called to someone's house because of disturbances. Carverdale wasn't the same as it was back then in the early '90s when the neighborhood was helping each other. Now the neighborhood seemed like they're against each other.

Acceptance

I still looked the same. I was 5'9", was brown skinned, had black hair, and was still slim. Both of my ears were pierced, and I had a tongue ring. But still I was unhappy about myself. I just couldn't see why I was born disabled. I had a lot of friends and a lot of sex friends; but just seeing myself in the mirror every day made me unhappy, upset, and abandoned from everyone else in the world, yes, abandoned! Abandoned from the world. Abandoned from family. Abandoned from friends.

And abandoned from myself.

I wanted to change myself so bad. That's why every so often when people saw me, I was changing my haircut, the way I dressed, and my attitude. Truth be told, I still felt bad about myself.

Every time I went to the mall or went anywhere, I saw these pretty boys, and I started to hurt inside. How many of you know you can be pretty on the outside but ugly on the inside? So if you're ugly on the outside, then you might be pretty on the inside. We are all unique in our own little way.

So we need to learn how to accept ourselves and believe it daily. When I was a child, when I was teenager, and even when I became an adult, I didn't know how to accept myself. All my life I thought life wasn't fair. But one thing now that I know for sure, what give your thoughts power are the emotions you put behind it. If you feel negative, then you will think negative, then you will be negative. It's time to start accepting yourself and believe it daily.

During this time, I was really close to my father. Every time I had one of my dizzy spells and I woke up in the hospital bed, my father was always there by my side. He helped me buy my first car. He helped me when he cosigned for my first house. So my father and I had a good relationship. As for my mother, we were a little distant. She still lived out of town and was still married to David G. I didn't talk to her much, but hi and bye. Don't get me wrong, I love my mother, but I distance myself from her.

Kelly and I were really close. We had our fights, but we got over them very quickly. Kim and I always fought. We weren't close, but we loved each other. My little sister Brazil was one person I loved dearly. Believe it or not, I looked up to her. Once again, she was strong, pretty, and smart—everything I wanted to be. And my brother Ken was there. That's all he was, just there. He moved around a lot. That's why my nephew Mark stayed with my father for a while.

I believed my little sister Brazil formed a prison mind with her lifestyle. Brazil was about fifteen years old when homosexuality became a part of her life. She said she had never been touched, or no one ever messed with her in any way when she was younger. She said it was just a part of her, and that's just how she felt. She was hiding it from us. But for some reason, I knew she had been captive through the homosexuality prison mind. How did I know? Maybe because homosexuality took over me too.

I started working in Banks School District as a student specialist. I was working with disabled children and loving the work I did. I remember working with this one young man named Robert. He was very special to me. He couldn't see, but he knew who you were by the sound of your voice and the feel of his hands. He wasn't a bad child. He just felt like he was alone at times.

My job was to make a difference in kids' lives and put a smile on their faces when they felt like they didn't have anyone else to depend on. For Robert, that's what I did. I remember at times when I came to work and walked in the classroom, Robert will hear my voice, and his face will light up. That brought joy to my heart. Robert was one of the kids who made me feel right about myself, but at times my prison mind would take the best of me.

As I looked back over my life and I thought things over, I wanted to change my prison mind. But that's all I knew. I was afraid of change. I am here to tell you if you are afraid to change for the better, don't be. You are safe; it's only change. I am safe; it's only change.

My sex addiction got worse. Time after time I felt depressed, lonely, confused, and hurt. So I would call up one of my lady friends and bring them to my house to have sex. And for some reason, if my lady friends couldn't come over, I would find myself watching sex movies. At times we attempt to live our lives based on our beliefs. That's what I did. I believed sex was my painkiller.

So I lived my life as sex being my drug and my friend.

Face Your Fears

I had a lot of fears growing up. But my fears became a part of me as I became an adult. My fears trapped me in a place that I was comfortable in. I was afraid of being by myself. I was scared to let go of my past so I can have a bright future. I was horrified to trust fully in God. I was doubtful of change. And I was fearful of living a new life and leaving my pain behind. It's time to start saying to ourselves, "Today is a new day, and I am a new me." It's time to start facing our fears.

My early experience of being fear-driven taught me when trouble comes, fear is not my best friend. Fear can handicap us from moving toward our goal in life.

Why are you troubled, and why do
doubts rise in your minds? (Luke 24:38)

Jesus said this to his disciples when he appeared in a locked room after his crucifixion. Jesus's disciples were frightened, thinking they saw a ghost. Fear overtook them. Fear has been trying to overtake me all my life. And all this time until now I couldn't hear God say, "Trust me."

I have told you these things, so that
in me you may have peace. In this world
you will have trouble. But take heart! I
have overcome the world. (John 16:33)

In spite of the fears, troubles, and struggles that we would face, Jesus is telling us we would not be alone. Jesus will never abandon us from our pain, fears, troubles, and struggles. We have to realize that the ultimate victory has already been won. We have to claim peace! We have to claim the victory!

We have to claim joy in Jesus Christ when our fears show up.

It is clear to see that Jesus said we are going to go through tribulations. But trusting in his presence and his power is the peacemaker to our fears.

Now don't get me wrong, a person who fears nothing loves nothing. And if you love nothing, then what joy do you have in your life? That means it's okay to fear, but don't let fear control you. Fear God! Not the things of this world. It's time to stand up and face our fears. Revelation 2:10 says,

> Do not be afraid of what you are
> about to suffer. I tell you, the devil will
> put some of you in prison to test you, and
> you will suffer persecution for ten days.
> Be faithful, even to the point of death,
> and I will give you the crown of life.

In 2004, Jasper and I were still best friends. We did everything together. We would go bowling, we would to the movies, and we would go out to eat. Jasper and I were like white on rice. Also, DeDe and I became real close friends too. She was a person I can talk to. I didn't tell her too much about the prison mind I was facing, because she also looked up to me. And I didn't want to let her down with my pain and sufferings. DeDe, along with everyone else, always came to me for help; so I couldn't let her down by showing her my pain.

I still was playing the drums at Ridge Chapel AME Church. Brother Kyle G. and I still went to other churches and played. Brother Kyle and I were a team in music. Brother Kyle can play the hell out of a bass guitar. We had a lot of fun lifting up the name of Jesus through musicals and workshops.

I thought I was living a good life because I was helping others, going to church, and doing all I can to be seen. But I wasn't close to God like I should have been.

> But as for me, it is good to be near
> God. (Psalm 74:28)

Beauty, love, and pleasure are all good things; but they're not the best. In fact, loving God, and making him our friend for life, is the best.

> The thief comes only to steal and
> kill and destroy; I have come that they
> may have life and have it to the fullest.
> (John 10:10)

The thief takes life; Jesus gives life. The life Jesus gives is abundantly richer. Now we have to take our life back from the thief because he means us no good. Let's draw near to God because Jesus is the good shepherd.

CHAPTER 23

Carverdale had two parks, which we called the big park and the little park. They built a community center at the little park where we had all kinds of events. Also, that's where they started having the Reading Program year-round.

The summer of 2004, I was a counselor at Carverdale Community Center for a summer camp program. I believed I really made a difference in those kids' lives. The reason I said that is because I was there when they needed someone to talk to. I was the only counselor who interacted with the children, and there were only three counselors.

One week we had this famous painter come by, and we had the kids paint a mural on the wall for the community center. It was fun! At the end of the week, the kids presented the mural in front of the community. The director was giving a speech of special thanks. As he was thanking staff members by name and the children for their hard work, the director forgot about me. As the director kept on talking, the kids all stood up and said, "What about Mr. Josh? He has done more for us than anyone else!" Then they looked back at me and smiled. That brought tears to my eyes.

I remember another time where the other two counselors left me at the community center with at least twenty kids by myself. So I had the kids play handball in the recreation area. We were having so much fun. But I started to feel really dizzy. So I knew right then my dizzy spells came back. I left the recreation area and went into my office. The next thing I knew, I passed out.

What I was told was the oldest child who was at the community summer camp program watched me walk into my office and saw me pass out. She ran into my office and started fanning me. While she was doing that, she was calming the other children down after they noticed what was going on. Then she called her mother, and she called 911. She took real good care of me until the other counselors and the ambulance came.

Willing to Change

The next day I woke up with a big box of get-well letters from all the kids from the summer camp. That made me feel loved. I walked into the doors of the community center going to pick up my check. The children noticed me walking in, and they all ran toward me and gave me a big hug. My boss gave me a few days off, but the kids wanted me to come back immediately. At that point, I knew I was so loved, and it made me feel good inside. But my prison mind wouldn't let me change my way of thinking.

We have to start telling ourselves, "I am willing to change." If the change is for the better, then say, "I am willing to change." Stop allowing your prison mind to trap you into that way of bad thinking. If you say, "I can't," change your thoughts to "I can."

One of the steps to being set free is to "believe." You have to believe and have faith that you can break free from that bad habit. You have to believe you are beautiful. You have to believe that "you can," instead of "you can't." I didn't believe I can change my way of thinking.

I didn't believe anyone cared. I didn't believe I was loved. But those children showed me someone does care and loves me. But my prison mind just didn't let me see it. I allowed my prison mind to keep me hostage.

I painted my future with bad thoughts of my past. It's time to accept the fact that every time you think of something, you are painting a picture of your future no matter if you are thinking good or bad.

By the end of the 2004 summer camp program, I gave most of the children my cell number, and I told them if they ever needed someone to talk to, they can call me. What I meant when I said "they can call me" is if they ran into any problems or needed help with their homework, they can call me. Stuff like that. Not just to call to have a friendly talk. Well, the night before the last day of the camp, the young lady who took care of me when I had my dizzy spells that one day called me. When I picked up, at first, I didn't know who it was; but when I noticed who it was, I asked her if she had a problem.

She said, "No, I just wanted to see what you are doing."

I told her, "You just can't call to be calling. That's not why I gave you my number." Her mother came into her room, I guess, and asked her who she was talking to.

She said, "Mr. Josh."

Her mother told her to hang up the phone.

The next day her mother called my boss. My boss talked to me and told me I couldn't give my number to the children and so on. Someone from the Carverdale community heard about it and took it out of context. That's when people started giving me a bad name, if you know what I mean.

In 2005, I started a children's choir in Carverdale. My little sister Brazil was helping me. This children's choir was really good. Their voices were out of this world. We also sang at musicals and workshops. They were so good they sang at a Black History Program at one of the Banks schools. Everyone really did enjoy the children's choir. Carverdale children's choir raised money so they can have a lock-in at one of the Carverdale churches. That was the first lock-in Carverdale ever had. We had a lot of fun. I was just trying to keep the kids off the streets and out of trouble.

Sometime in 2005, my mother moved back to Houston because she divorced her husband, David. I don't know what happened in their marriage, but I was glad my mother moved back to Houston. My prison mind of sex was still there. I was having girlfriends after girlfriends.

Love

What is love? I didn't know what love really was back then. Most of all the girlfriends I had I didn't love. I used to think love wouldn't find me. So what is love?

> Love is patient, love is kind. It does not envy, it does not boast, it is not proud. It is not rude, it is not self-seeking, it is not easily angered, it keeps no record of wrongs. (1 Corinthians 13:4–5)

I used to feel like I wasn't loved. It wasn't because I didn't believe in love. I just didn't know what love really was. I didn't know love could be healthy for you. True love will set you free. Do you remember the story in the Bible in John 11:38–44 where Jesus raised Lazarus from the dead? When Jesus came to the tomb, he said, "Take away the stone." When they moved the stone, Jesus said in a loud voice, "Lazarus, come out!" When Lazarus came out, he was wrapped with strips of linen, and a cloth was covering his face. Jesus commanded, "Take off the grave cloths and let him go." Jesus said that so Lazarus could be free to walk.

It was the love that Jesus had for Lazarus that raised him from the dead. We need that same kind of freedom. And Jesus wants us to have it. It's time to start telling our dead and bad habits that trap us and hold us captive, "In Jesus's name, let me go! I'm putting sex, drugs, stealing, stress, depression, and all the things that lock me up in my prison mind behind me. It's time for me to live the life of love!" Even today sometimes I'm still struggling with love. Like for starters, "Love your enemies."

The middle of 2005, the Gospel Twinz were doing really good with their music. We would practice just about every day when they got home from school and finished their homework. Will and Mary practiced with us. The twins had no time for trouble because I was always guiding them on the right road. They had a hardworking mother, and their father wasn't really around, so I was there for them. I stayed on them when their grades were low. I stayed on them when they thought about the word "trouble." But through it all, they were good boys. I was happy because I was doing something good for the twins.

The twins tried their best to stay out of trouble, but sometimes Will would start up a lot of mess among the group. When it's practice time, Will would be lazy and want to take all kinds of breaks. The twins, Ashley, and I got tired of dealing with Will's mess; so we voted and kicked him out of the group. I'm not trying to put Will down, but he was standing in our way of us trying to make it big.

After Will got out of the group, the twins and Mary started to get back on the right path. Later in 2005, the Gospel Twinz started going to the studio to record their first CD. It was so exciting to watch them rap in the studio. You see, we had a lot of challenges in our lives. Even when I wanted to give up, the twins pushed me to keep on going. My prison mind tried to stop me on the path of righteousness, but the twins lifted me back up. One thing you have to know, there are challenges through your paths of life, but don't give up. Just keep going.

At the end of 2005, I realized I was having conflicts with Satan. I wanted to do right, but I know I was doing wrong. I wanted to follow Christ, but I was going the direction of Satan. My mind was getting the best of me. I just didn't know what to do. Now I know when I face battles with Satan, I should not fear him but instead stay focused on Christ who I know will win the victory every time.

I helped everyone in need, but why couldn't I just help myself? That didn't make sense to me. The summer of 2005, I worked at New Day Camp helping disabled children. That was the same camp I went to when I was young. I mentored a lot of children. I did a lot around the church and in Carverdale. So why couldn't I just get my mind right? Why couldn't I break free from my prison mind? I believed in God, but I was lost. I was like a sheep trying to find my way back home.

Every time I felt that pain or thought about my past when I was young, I needed to take my drug to make me feel better. Sex did that for me, but sometimes I couldn't find anyone to have sex with, so I started playing with myself all the time, even if I just had sex with someone. My prison mind blocked me from a lot of things such as when I did feel pain or hurt, my prison mind kept me from turning to God; instead, I turned to sex.

CHAPTER 24

A Change Is Gonna Come

This is a journey, a journey of life and
    beauty,
As you pass the mountains, lakes, rivers,
    and ocean.
I have to set myself to the right position,
To a beautiful dream the way it seems.
Beyond the point where I can see clear,
Where it's no fear that I will have
A possibility and the right opportunity
To see life as a free soul in everything
    that it holds.
I can't even control my reaction
And open my eyes so I can pay attention.
I see the waterfall as I hear its call
It's calling, "Peace be with you in every-
    thing you do."
I believe this is paradise,
Man, it's wonderful and it's nice.
This is the center of a new century and
    it's God who only holds the right
    key.
I can even hear my heart telling me this
    is a chapter of a new start.

As I deposit myself to make this change.
There is no one that can make it
rearrange.
As the sky is blue and the clouds are
white.
There was something in the sky that
caught my sight.
It was a system of recreation,
And full of life of fighting temptations.
As the birds sing,
I see the animals coming from the other
side of the river stream.
From the tall trees and the green grass,
It must be spring. I want this image,
This image to last.
Do you see this?
Now this is something you don't want to
miss.
The streets are made of gold and now my
life is starting to unfold.
Let me transfer this so that you can
understand.
Don't let anyone tell you,
"You can't change."
Yes, you can because you are God's right-
hand man.
Is this the label that means God is able?
I can call this my testimony…
That a change is gonna come!

Lost vs. Freedom Part 2

In 2006, I was working for this lady named Sister G., who happened to be Suzanne's grandmother. Sister G. opened up a mission many years ago for homeless women and children who needed someone to love. Sister G. also adopted twenty-four children who needed someone to love.

They are grown now. When I got hired to work for Sister G., I worked with this little boy named Keith. Before I became his mentor, he had other mentors. Keith's mentors gave up on him because he was a troubled child. His grades were always low. His conduct couldn't get any better. People told me there was no hope for that boy. But I never gave up on Keith. The reason is because people were always in and out of his life. I didn't want to be one of those people. Yes, Keith gave me hell at first. Then when God allowed Keith to trust me, that's when things changed for the better.

Keith's grades got better; his conduct became better. His teachers were like "I don't know how Josh did it, but Keith was like a new kid." It was the trust that Keith and I had with each other. I always had hope for Keith, and I was not going to give up. Keith always wanted to be around me. I kept a smile on his face.

I also was hired to work with Sister G.'s youngest daughter, Max. Max was also a troubled child. Her real mother gave her up to Sister G. when Max was just a baby. Max had so much hate in her heart. She didn't get along with anyone. She gave me so much hell, but once again I didn't give up on her.

I worked with Max when she allowed me to. Max had a passion for music. So I taught her how to play the drums. She was pretty good at it. Then Max started going to church with me. Slowly but surely, Max was coming around. One thing

Max had a problem with was running the streets. Max loved staying out late. It made Sister G. crazy.

Choices

We as people have a choice to do what we want no matter if it's good or bad. I made a choice to stay stuck in my prison mind of the past. You see, when you're not a Christian, you have no choices, because most of the time you will go the way of evil. But when you become a Christian, God gives you free will—free will to follow him or free will to follow Satan. Some think it's easier to not have that choice. I made a choice for sex to be my drug. Personal power is a choice. I choose my behavior. My life is my responsibility. That's the way we need to start thinking.

I made people responsible for my problems. I blamed them because of my past. We have to stop looking at others as if they put the load of problems on us. It's time to change your thinking because personal weakness is also a choice. Saying, "My life is *not* my responsibility," is how we shouldn't think.

For a long time, I blamed God for making me the way I am. I didn't think my life was my responsibility because God made me different. So I thought I can do whatever I wanted and not be punished by God or by anyone here on earth. I had a choice to do right and to not be a sex addict. My choice of being a sex addict became worse than I thought.

My baby girl Suzanne, the twins, DeDe, Mary, Max, and I became one big happy family. We did everything together. People would always see us around each other. There was not a day that went by that people wouldn't see us hanging with each other. DeDe and I took Max under our wings, and she became our daughter.

Don't get me wrong, we all had our problems. We sometimes would get mad at each other, but we would always find a way to fix it. DeDe, the twins, Mary, and Max were always there for me; and I thank God for them.

My prison mind was getting the best of me. I was getting STD after STD. Having sex with girls after girls. Was I that messed up about my emotional pain to where I didn't care about the physical pain? It's time to point out the truths. I was digging a hole I couldn't get myself out of.

Around 2006, my little sister Brazil started coming out about being gay. When she did, she was pushing herself away from me. We stopped hanging out and doing things together. We would always fight and not speak to each other for days. That hurt me so much. I can remember a time when we were so close. Now it seems like we were too far apart. If she only knew I looked up to her.

In the middle of 2006, people from the Carverdale community started really giving me a bad name. The reason was because of what happened when I gave those kids at the community center my phone number. And also, every time they saw me, I was hanging around kids. That was just the work I loved to do. Helping those kids so they wouldn't be stuck in a prison mind like myself.

I believed people were jealous of me, and they were always putting me down instead of encouraging me. God has blessed me with all of these children. I say I wanted to make a difference in their lives, but truly they made a difference in my life. I just wished everyone would have seen that. Working with all of these kids made me realize not to ever give up on myself.

There is hope in everyone. The twins taught me that.

I started to dislike the people in Carverdale. They made me feel so bad for the work that I was doing. All I wanted was to help children. So this hatred that was developing in my heart was making me not want to care anymore. How in the hell did I make enemies who could eat me up and spit me out?

One of the truths that I discovered about myself was that I really like helping kids because they made me feel wanted. They accepted me for who I was. That alone made me feel good. While all the adults were turning up their noses at me, the kids were always lifting me up.

Sinful Nature

I know I had a very sinful nature. My sins made me a prisoner. These sins were taking over my life. Galatians 5:19–21 says,

> The acts of the sinful nature are obvious: sexual immorality, impurity and debauchery; idolatry and witchcraft; hatred, discord, jealousy, fits of rage, selfish ambition, dissensions, factions and envy; drunkenness, orgies, and the like.

All of us have evil desires; we can't ignore them. We must deal with them by crucifying them (Galatians 5:24). I had sex, and I started to feel envy toward people. I was jealous of my little sister Brazil, and I had fits of rage. I ignored these sins. They didn't matter to me at that time. I allowed them to put me in that prison mind. It's clear to see I wasn't trying to transform my life. Those who refuse to deal with such sins won't receive the gift of the Holy Spirit, which will help them transform their life.

Fruits of the Spirit

Let's talk about the fruits of the spirit that we all need to have in our life. The fruits of the spirit will transform you out of that sinful nature.

> But the fruit of the spirit is love, joy, peace, patience, kindness, goodness, faithfulness, gentleness and self-control. Against such things there is no law. Those who belong to Christ Jesus have crucified the sinful nature with its passions and desires. (Galatians 5:22–24)

I was trying to find that peace and joy. I believed I had the love, but I knew I wasn't patient. Even today I have problems on being patient. There is a spiritual battle going on between our sinful desires and the Holy Spirit. You have evil vs. good, destructive vs. productive, self-centered vs. self-giving, sinful vs. holy, and deadly vs. abundant life. Which of these qualities do you want the spirit to produce in you? You decide!

A lot of people believe that in time your pain will heal. I believe that's not true. Time has passed, but the scars of your past remain. Someone once said this, "It has been said, 'Time heals all wounds.' I do not agree. The wounds remain. In time, the mind, (protecting its sanity) covers them with scar tissue and the life lessons. But it's never gone." Remember this, no man is rich enough to buy back the past. The future is purchased by the past! That means you can't change the past, but let your past lessons help you become a better person in the future.

CHAPTER 25

The twins always spent the night on the weekends at my house with my baby girl Suzanne. They really enjoyed staying at my house. We would go to the movies, go swimming, and go skating. Suzanne enjoyed their company. The twins would look forward to the times we spent together for the weekends. The twins were like my little brothers; they looked up to me helping others.

The year 2007 was the hardest and most stressful year of my life. I'll get to that later in this chapter. I was working at the House of Joy at Sister G.'s mission. I was an assistant coordinator helping kids through a tutor program. The joy I put on their faces made me feel so good. When I was not at the House of Joy for whatever reason, my boss, Ms. T., would tell me, "The kids had been asking for you all day." And once I stepped foot into the House of Joy's front doors, the children all came running and giving me a big hug, telling me how much they missed me. I evidently was doing something right because those kids were full of joy.

February of 2007, I had some so-called friends over to my house. I went to the restroom, and one of them went into my room and stole my checks. I didn't find out until the bank called me one day and said someone was trying to cash $1,000 in my name. So when I found out who it was, I was going to turn them into the cops.

Mary was seventeen years old at the time, and she always stayed in trouble. Her family just about gave up on her. Mary was in and out of jail. She was stealing, gangbanging, and doing other stuff (I can't say). People were always telling me to stop trying to help Mary because she was hopeless. But I knew one day Mary would change her life. When Mary was seventeen, she got kicked out of her mother's house for whatever reason. Mary was homeless and living on the streets. When she got a chance, she was moving from house to house. I felt bad for her because I knew deep down inside, she was a good person.

So I let Mary move in with me. Everyone thought I was crazy for doing such a thing. But like I said before, I was not going to give up on her. People turned their backs on Mary, even her own family. Yes, Mary was a troublemaker. Yes, Mary dropped out of school. But all she needed was a little push and for people to care for her. I was someone who encouraged her. When Mary was living with me, she got a job. She wanted to go back to school. Overall, she was doing good. By the grace of God, she was doing what she needed to do. All she needed was someone to show her that love. I gave her that love. So she never gave up.

For some reason, my pain of the past was hindering me. A few months after Mary moved in my house, I found myself having sex with her. I'm not going to talk too much about it so I won't be putting Mary out there. But I can say this: Mary was also gay.

In the summer of 2007, my cousin Lize was having problems at her mom's house. So Lize came to stay with me. In the process of her staying with me, we became close. Lize became my favorite cousin. Don't get me wrong, I still love Starr, but she wasn't my favorite cousin anymore.

I helped a lot of people throughout the years. Helping people is something I love to do. God gave me that gift, I believe. The funny thing was I had a lot of enemies. Now I guess you're thinking, *You've done all this good, and you have enemies?* Yes! I have enemies. Most people didn't like what I was doing because God gave me these gifts. I wasn't doing it for the spotlight anymore. I was doing it because I really cared. But for some reason, people didn't approve. So people started slandering my name, giving my character a bad taste. Let's stop here for a moment. Remember when I said earlier "2007 was the hardest and most stressful year of my life"? Well, sit back and listen to the reason.

The Harvest Year of My Life

Early Friday morning on October 11, 2007, police officers kicked down my door. I got arrested for a crime that I didn't commit. Will and his family lied on me and said I molested him back in 2002 when he was eight or nine. I believe Will's story wasn't making any sense, and the cops weren't believing it. So Will told them about the game we played with the twins back in 2002. Now I was charged with the twins as well. The court did not have any evidence or witnesses to convict me of any crime. So why did I get arrested in the first place?

While I was in the cops' car, I was thinking to myself, *Why would Will do this to me?* Reasons started popping up into my head. Will was mad at the twins and me for kicking him out of our group. Then I thought, *Well, ever since I was about to put one of those so-called friends Keke, Mercy, and London in jail for stealing my checks out my room when I was roommates with Keke. London's mother was friends with Will's mother who I think put Will up to this lie about me because I was about to put her son in jail.* And what made me come up with this conclusion was because almost every day Will would go to the little park in Carverdale with his mother's friend, and they would be sitting there and messing with the other people at the park. They would try to get people to fight.

If Will was mad at me, why did he put the twins in it? This changed our lives. We stopped rapping for the moment. The twins even told the cops that nothing was going on. "Josh wasn't messing with us." People at this time were determined to put me away. My family and friends were mad and upset. The people I worked with just couldn't understand this lie. All this time that I worked with children, none of them said I messed with them in any way.

I stayed in the county jail for three months, and I was really mad at God. I didn't know why he would allow this to happen to me. My prison mind started going into all kinds of directions. My faith was very little.

Coping with Your Problems

I prayed and I prayed, and God was nowhere to be found. I didn't know how to cope with my problems. And now I really needed God to help.

> In the same way, the spirit helps us
> in our weakness. We do not know what
> we ought to pray for, but the spirit himself
> intercedes for us with groans that words
> cannot express. And he who searches
> our hearts knows the mind of the spirit,
> because the spirit intercedes for the saints

in accordance with God's will. (Romans
8:26–27)

When you become a believer, you don't have to depend on your own resources to cope with your problems. When you don't know the right words to pray, the Holy Spirit will do it for you and with you. And God will answer. We don't need to be afraid to come to God. Ask the Holy Spirit to help you and let it be God's will. Then trust that God will do what is best for you.

That was my problem. I didn't trust God fully.

CHAPTER 26

January 2, 2008, I bonded out of the county jail after three months. The DA indicted me with four charges: aggravated sexual assault of a child with Will, two counts of sexual performance by a child with Will and Luck, and indecency with a child with Larry. So as you can see, they were trying to nail me to the cross. I had never been in trouble like this before. I really didn't know what to do.

Two days after I bonded out, I had to appear to court for the charges. When I stood before the judge, I didn't have a lawyer. The judge told me the next time I come in her courtroom without a lawyer, she would put me back in jail. That scared me. The Lord knew I didn't want to end up back in that place.

After I got out of jail, I stayed with my mother because my family didn't want me to go back to Carverdale where Will lived and so I wouldn't have any problems. I still went to Ridge Chapel AME Church on Sundays, even though Ridge was in Carverdale. My pain started to come back fast. Then my prison mind became my best friend. I needed my drugs. I had to start making new friends, so I got on the chat line. I would meet girls after girls, and we would have sex to get my mind off my situation.

Finally, I hired a lawyer my mother hooked me up with. Her name was Ms. C., and she said she was a Christian woman, so that was a plus. I kept going back and forth to court on the charges. The DA was trying to find more evidence on me to build their case. I wanted people to know I didn't do anything. The DA couldn't find any bad things on me.

When I was going to Carverdale to see my father and to attend church, people would look at me funny. This case really messed me up. I lost my house, and I was about to lose my job. Suzanne went back to live with her mother. My life really turned upside down. Don't get me wrong, a lot of people knew I wouldn't do anything like that. The twins' mother trusted me and believed in me that I wasn't messing with her kids. The twins even told her that Will lied.

My mother had a boyfriend at this time, and she was getting ready to move in with him. So I went back to Carverdale to live with my father. I really thank God for my father because he is a good father. My father spent so much money on me trying to clear my name; it was amazing. My father didn't know if I did this crime or not, but he stood by my side the whole time. This case messed up my family's life, but God was getting us through it. My prison mind was blocking me of seeing the goodness of God.

If you notice throughout this book, I never mentioned that I had a birthday party. The reason was because ever since I was young, I never had one. Brazil, Kelly, Kim, and Ken all had birthday parties when they were young, I believe. I always wondered why I never had one when I was a child. So that was another reason I always felt left out.

The DA was trying to keep me away from the twins, but the twins' mother would allow me to hang out at their house. She would let me mentor them. June 22, 2008, the twins, their mother, and their sister DeDe gave me my first real birthday party. I was so happy, and I really did feel so loved. Everyone was there—my sisters, my friends, and my cousin Lize. My sister Brazil was dating this woman named PG; she was also there. PG was like my sister-in-law because she and Brazil had been dating for a long time.

I had a good time at my party, and I saw a lot of people who believed in me and knew I didn't do what I was charged with. I was going through a very hard time, and I really wanted to give up.

But the twins and everyone who was at my party gave me a little hope.

A Night That Turned Bad

Let me give you a little background and insight on one of my best friends. Ever since I met DeDe, she had been bisexual. Throughout the years, she was dating boys and girls. In 2008, DeDe had this one girlfriend named Toya. Toya was pretty cool. DeDe had been dating Toya for at least two years off and on. One day DeDe just didn't want to be with Toya anymore. That's when problems started to happen in her life.

Toya would go to DeDe's mother's house trying to fight DeDe. We would have to call the cops all the time on Toya. In July or August of 2008, I was sitting in the twins' driveway talking on the phone about 8:00 p.m. The twins' mother was at work. There were a lot of kids at the twins' house playing. I asked DeDe and Mary and her girlfriend to walk these kids home because it was getting late.

On their way back to the house, Toya and her sister jumped out of their car. Toya was trying to fight DeDe, and Toya's sister was trying to fight Max. Larry, one of the twins, confronted Toya, trying to talk to her. Even though DeDe was the big sister, Larry was trying to be the bigger brother.

Toya didn't want to hear it. Then Toya pulled out a fish knife and stabbed Larry right in the liver. Then Toya and her sister jumped back in their car and drove off. By the time the twins, DeDe, Max, Mary, and her girlfriend got back to our street on Porto Rico, I heard a loud scream.

It was Mary's girlfriend, so I dropped the phone and ran toward them. Larry was lying in the middle of the street bleeding nonstop. One thing I can say for sure, Larry was very strong because he didn't cry. Or maybe he was just in shock.

All of us were so mad, screaming. We called 911. I called my father, and he ran down the street to where we were to help. I got on my knees and grabbed a hold of Larry's hand, and I said, "I don't care what the DA says. I'm going to be there when you wake up." Larry was losing so much blood. I cried out to God asking him to let Larry live. I was so mad at God. He allowed me to go through these charges, and now he's letting this happen to an innocent kid. It just wasn't fair! What was God trying to tell me?

The twins' family, my sister Brazil, Mary and her girlfriend Max, and I were waiting at the hospital until Larry came out of surgery. I kept my word when I told Larry I will be right by his side when he wakes up. When Larry opened his eyes, I was right there. Tears were falling down my face because God kept him there.

All these things were happening in my life, and I just didn't know what to do. I was losing my faith, and my pain was taking over. I prayed and I prayed, but it seems like God wasn't there. I was beginning to be weak, but I needed God to make me strong.

In July of 2008, Mary said she was raped by her godfather; and around that time, Mary and I were still having sex unprotected. Mary ended up pregnant. My sister Kim was one month pregnant too.

Larry was recovering from being stabbed. We all were happy Larry was okay. Toya did go to jail, but I don't know what the outcome was. The DA had to reschedule me from going to court until Larry became a 100 percent better. My lawyer, Ms. C., was lazy. She did some things, but the only time she called me was when she wanted her money.

In September of 2008, I had a big musical at my church Ridge Chapel. It was very nice. My mother and my aunt Karen, Kelly and her boyfriend, my brother, my sister Kim, and my sister Brazil were there. Throughout the years I was rapping, that was my mother's first time ever coming to one of my musicals. That put a smile on my face. Larry did make a 100 percent recovery, and the Gospel Twinz did perform that night.

The Real Change

Finally, January of 2009, the DA dropped the charges of the twins. The DA called the twins' mother and my sister Brazil to bring the twins into their office. The DA asked all of them some questions, and the DA decided to drop all charges of the twins if I sign for probation of aggravated sexual assault of a child for Will. I talked to my lawyer; and even though I didn't do this crime, to make a long story short, my lawyer and the DA tricked me so I could be signed for probation.

Now I was on probation, and I couldn't be around any children. That means the Gospel Twinz was over. I couldn't be with them or my nephews at any time while I was on probation. That hurt me so much. I just didn't know why God would do this to me. I was hurting inside, so I needed my drug. All my life I felt alone. But this time I really felt like I was by myself.

On March 2, 2009, I got this crazy phone call. I reported it to my probation officer so I wouldn't get into trouble. The next thing I knew, I was going back to jail, but this time I was headed to prison. My mother was crying, and my father was upset. I didn't do anything wrong.

So why was I going to prison?

I was trying to trust God, but my faith was getting lost. My family and friends were telling me to keep my head up. At that time, they didn't know how I felt. I was mad as hell at God because he didn't help me when I was calling him. I was like "What is the point of living now?" I thought he turned his back on me. I'm not going to lie—yes, I was giving up. That's what Satan wanted. He wanted me to give up and turn away from God. Do you feel like giving up when times are hard? See, Satan wants us to worship him, so he would do anything to get our focus off God. Pray. Don't give in to Satan's lies.

At the age of twenty-three, I thought I was free. But now I was locked up in jail thinking, *What the hell!* as I was sitting in Harris County while my mother came to see me week after week. She tried to stay strong, but deep down inside I believe my mother was feeling weak. My church family and my real friends wrote me letters of grief. I was already feeling low, under, and beneath. The judge ordered me six years, and now I got to watch my mother behind a glass window with her eyes full of pain and tears. I was on my way to prison with the judge's decision. I wanted to give up because my mind was corrupt.

CHAPTER 27

May 5, 2009, I was on the bus going to prison. I didn't know what to do. I was so scared. I felt like I wasn't going to make it out of prison alive. It was my first time in prison. What should I do? All I wanted was to just help people. And now I see helping people got me into prison, or so I thought.

Forgiveness

My prison mind got me to the point where I wanted to hate Will bad. He did me wrong, and he hurt my family. I thought there was no way I can ever forgive him. Now my whole life was messed up because of Will. All this time I trapped myself in the state of mind of no return. When someone does you wrong, do you forgive them? The Bible tells us to overcome evil with good. I didn't know how to do that. My freedom was just taken away.

> Do not take revenge, my friends, but leave room for God's wrath, for it is written: "It is mine to avenge; I will repay," says the Lord. On the contrary "If your enemy is hungry, feed him; if he is thirsty, give him something to drink. In doing this, you will heap burning coals on his head." Do not be overcome by evil

but overcome evil with good. (Romans 12:19–21)

Remember, grace is on our side. When we give our enemies something to drink and feed them, we are not excusing their sins to us; but we are recognizing them, forgiving them, and loving them no matter what they did to us—just like Christ did for us.

For the first year in prison, I just couldn't forgive Will for what he had done to me. I didn't trust God enough to give him all of my problems. Paul said, "Forgive our enemies."

Forgiveness breaks cycles, forgiveness makes our enemies feel ashamed, and it may change their ways. And if your enemies don't accept your forgiveness, that's okay, because by forgiving them, it will set you free from that prison mind of unforgiveness.

Yes, it's difficult to forgive someone who did you wrong. But try to respond with kind actions and lend your enemies a helping hand. You will see that right actions lead to right feelings. The best way to stop your enemies is to turn them into friends. Even today I have a problem of forgiving my enemies, but with God's help, he will place forgiveness in my heart. For about two and a half years, I couldn't forgive Will and his family. Evil thoughts always went through my mind. All this time I didn't know I trapped myself in my own prison mind. God was trying to tell me something when I was in the world, but I wasn't listening. It took me to come to an actual prison to know that it's time for my prison mind to be set free.

God has opened my eyes to forgive and love my enemies. Like I said, it was hard before, and today I'm still struggling with that forgiveness. Luke 6:27–28 says,

But I tell you who hear me: Love your enemies, do good to those who hate

you, bless those who curse you, pray for
those who mistreat you.

So that's what I started doing: praying, loving, and blessing Will and his family, as well as everyone else who didn't like me because of whatever they didn't like about me.

Before I go on, my sister Kim had my niece Sandy on March 19, 2009. And Mary had her son Daniel on April 6, 2009. Today, we don't know if Daniel is my child, but we will find out when I get out of prison.

God does things for many reasons. God didn't put me in prison, but he allowed me to come to prison to open my eyes to my evil desires. And my sex addiction was one of these evil desires. I was loved all this time, but I blocked myself from seeing that. The Jews looked down on the Romans because they were doing wrong to God's people. But Jesus told the Jews to love these enemies. After Jesus said such things, many turned away from Christ. Jesus wasn't saying have affection for your enemies; Jesus was talking about praying for them, thinking of ways to help them. It is an act of will.

Jesus loves us, even though we at times turn against God. We need to follow Jesus's example by loving our enemies. Have respect for your enemies as you want for yourself.

It's time to start healing yourself. It's time to start writing your own story. We need to change the rest of our story. Each chapter doesn't have to be repetitive as it has been in our life experiences. So therefore, it's time to change your story. Take the pen back from Satan and write your own story. Satan has written enough. You can't rewrite those chapters, but you can control what you do with the information written in those chapters. Your story will help keep your memories of God's faithfulness alive in your life.

For a long time, I didn't love myself. I didn't know how to. Since I've been in prison, God has shown me many things, and he has blessed me in many ways. I'm starting a new life. If you feel the way I have felt when my prison mind blocked me from seeing God's goodness, it's time to say, "I love myself just the way I am." It's time to *leave your pain behind*. It's time to *reverse this curse*. And it's time to be *set free*.

It's 2014, and I'm still in prison. But don't worry because I get out on December 10. I'll be finished doing my time. Thank you, Jesus! I realize this was a lesson to be learned. God allowed me to come to prison so I can be *set free*. Now I know you are thinking, *How are you free and you are still in prison?* Well, I am free. I'm not crazy. You see, it took God to sit me down to open my eyes, and it took people to lie on me for me to come to prison because of all the good works I've done. God was just preparing me to live a better Christian life. Nobody can or will take this *freedom* away from me. I know I'm behind bars, but God has *set me free*, while my enemies are still trapped in their prison minds.

Now I am *free*!

CHAPTER 28

It's Time to Be Set Free

> It is for freedom that Christ has set
> us free. Stand firm, then, and do not let
> yourself be burdened again by a yoke of
> slavery. (Galatians 5:1)

The days of slavery are over. But we allow ourselves to become slaves in our own minds. We allow ourselves to be captive by darkness instead of trying to find the true light. There is true freedom, but you have to want it! You have to believe it! And for a Christian, if you want this freedom, you have to trust in God and put all your faith in him. That way all the locks will pop open from the chains that are holding you down. Worries, gone! Stress, gone! Depression, gone! Drugs, gone! Sex addiction, gone! And all the other stuff that is keeping your freedom away from you, gone!

And for the nonbelievers, you have to accept the Lord Jesus Christ as your personal Savior. You have to believe that he died for your sins and that he has set you free. True freedom is when Christ came to earth and died on the cross to set us free from sin. We are no longer in slavery. Yes, indeed, Christ came to rescue us from slavery and set us free. That doesn't mean we are free to do whatever we want to do, because if that was the case, we are putting ourselves back in slavery. When I was a child, I didn't really understand fully the things of God. But as I got older, I started to understand, but I didn't want to accept it. I already trapped myself in that prison mind to where I was stuck in my own ways. I accepted Christ in my life, but I didn't accept that freedom Christ gave me. I wanted to do whatever I wanted to do, and that is what put me into slavery and into my prison mind.

> You, my brothers, were called to be free. But do not use your freedom to indulge the sinful nature; rather, serve one another in love. (Galatians 5:13)

Paul is telling us the difference between freedom to sin and freedom to serve. Freedom to sin is no freedom at all because we become prisoners to Satan, or prisoners to our own sinful nature. As Christians, we should not be slaves to our sins because Christ gave us the freedom to do what's right, and to praise and lift up his name through loving service to others.

As you read about my life, you will see that I've been through a lot. I didn't trust God like I should have. I didn't allow him to set me free from my pain. I know what was right, but I was doing wrong. I was indulging into my sinful nature. I was feeling sorry for myself, and I was hurting myself and hurting others. I had the freedom to do the right things. But I became a slave to my thoughts, mind, and body. So God had to sit me down and open my eyes so that I can see the blessings he has stored for me. And when it became clear, I told myself, "It's time to come alive today!"

Come Alive

I realized that Christ wasn't the only one who has been resurrected. We as Christians are resurrected from the dead with Christ. When we first accepted Jesus Christ to be our Lord, that day we came alive. The old person inside of us died, and a new creature was born!

> Therefore, if anyone is in Christ, he
> is a new creation; the old has gone, the
> new has come! (2 Corinthians 5:17)

When we became Christians, we are new on the inside. The Holy Spirit gave us new life, and we are not the same anymore. Not only did we get transformed or reformed, but we were also recreated. We are one with Christ.

That means we have a new master, and we are no longer under Satan's control.

We are free from the chains that were holding us down. But you have to believe in that freedom.

Now I bet you are asking, "If we are so free, why can't I stop doing drugs? Why is my mother sick? Why do I have so much pain? Why? Why? Why?" It's easy—you are letting Satan convince you that he still controls you. You are letting Satan convince you that your spiritual man is still dead. It's time to come alive today! Now you are dead to sin and alive to Jesus's power.

The meaning of this book is to help the readers find that freedom before it's too late. Don't wait until you find yourself in an actual prison to realize you have been in your prison mind all your life. Or don't wait until you are on your last limb to know you have been held captive in your own mind. Jesus Christ has the key to open all doors and unlock all chains that your mind has created to keep you in bondage.

It's time to be *set free*!

Jesus has that *freedom*!

Reverse This Curse

There is a curse on this earth that happened many years ago. We all know the story about Adam and Eve. When Satan came to Eve, he had no power at all. So Satan came to her in the form of a serpent. Satan deceived Eve into disobeying God's command. Adam was not deceived, but since he was Eve's husband, he followed her.

Satan did not talk to Adam directly, but Adam was standing there when Satan was deceiving his wife. Adam should have stood up and kicked Satan out of the garden right then, but instead, he put aside God's command that was given to him, and he made Satan his lord.

> Christ redeemed us from the curse
> of the law by becoming a curse for us, for
> it is written, "Cursed is everyone who is
> hung on a tree." (Galatians 3:13)

I too was just like Adam. I bowed down to Satan and gave him authority over my life. I allowed Satan to be my ruler, just like Adam allowed Satan to be the ruler of the earth. And when Satan became my ruler and took authority over my life, that's when things changed.

> Therefore, just as sin entered the
> world through one man, and death
> through sin, and in this way, death came

to all men, because all sinned. (Romans
5:12)

Yes, I'm a Christian, but I made choices. Now I bet
you are wondering, "Will we be cursed forever? Can God
do something about this curse?" In fact, God already has
through Jesus. The day that you accept the Lord Jesus Christ
as your Lord, you are no longer under the leadership of Satan.
You are free from the curse. This doesn't mean that the curse
isn't out there in the world. We can still see it and hear it all
around us. But now you have a choice. You have the power in
Jesus's name to have victory over the curse. God has done his
part by sending Christ to free us from the curse. Now it's all
up to you to have that freedom of life.

Joshua's Four Steps on How to Start
the Process to Be Set Free

I noticed at this point in my life that something had
to change. I wanted to be free from my prison mind, but I
didn't know I was doing something wrong. My life was being
controlled by my fears. I was trying to serve God, but I was
doing things my own way.

I wasn't giving God my all. How many of you know that
you can't give 50 percent? You have to give God 100 percent.
God wants it all. If you want to be free, you have to give God
your all. It took me a while to learn and to understand that I
was trapped in my prison mind, and I needed God's help. I
had to stop letting Satan control me and control my thoughts.

So one day I realized that it was time for me to be *set free*.
God has opened my eyes to where I came up with these four
steps that started my process of being free. I hope and pray
that these steps can and will help you as these steps helped me.

First, you have to *change* your thinking. That means you have to change your thought process from "I can't" to "I can," from "negative" to "positive," from "bad" to "good," from "sad" to "happy."

Second, you have to *believe*. That means you have to believe that you are changing.

You have to believe you can do it and God will help you.

Third, *stop worrying* about your past. That means you can't be stuck in the past. You have to learn how to forgive yourself and others from your past. That doesn't mean to forget about your past but remember your past. That way when you overcome the things that happened in your past, you can look back at the past and say, "You thought you had me, but I overcame you!"

Finally, start *trusting* in God. That means to start putting your whole 100 percent in God and not 50 percent. You have to trust in God that he can, and he will help you change your situation. Now, don't get me wrong: I still struggle with a lot of things, but God will help me through all my problems. All I have to do is let go and let God, and my freedom will last. I pray that the readers learn, grow, and understand where I was coming from in this book, because your freedom is waiting for you!

Instruction on Christian Freedom

I told you about my four steps in starting the process of being set free. Now here are some true Christian freedom we all need to learn.

Now about food sacrificed to idols:
we know that we all possess knowledge.

> Knowledge puffs up, but love builds up.
> (1 Corinthians 8:1)

One of the most important steps of Christian freedom is *love*. Yes, indeed, knowledge makes us smart, but love will give us the power to move on. First, love God. Then you have to love yourself. Finally, love others. And the freedom that God gives you, you have to use it wisely. What I mean is God gives us free will. So now we have the freedom to choose between good and evil.

And as for the stronger believers, don't use the freedom that God gave you to prey on the weaker believers. As a stronger believer, we should help those who are struggling in their walk to try to find that freedom that the stronger believers have.

> Be careful, however, that the exercise
> of your freedom does not become a stum-
> bling block to the weak. (1 Corinthians 8:9)

Advice to the stronger believers: do not boast your freedom. Show love so you won't be a stumbling block to the weaker believers. And now advice to the weaker believers: even though you may feel like you have no freedom, pray to God, and ask him to show you the way to your freedom. Don't ever give up on God or yourself. Stay strong and faithful, and God will show you the way. To read more on Christian freedom, read all of 1 Corinthians 8.

Leaving the Pain Behind

When I say "leaving the pain behind," that doesn't mean forget about your past. Leaving the pain behind means don't dwell on your past but use your past as a lesson to build up your future. "What do you mean, Josh?" you may ask. You see, when you become successful, for example, and overcome your weakness like a drug addiction, you can look back and smile. As you're smiling, you can tell your past, "You thought you had me. You thought you can control me. But I just want you to know I made it through because God kept me."

> Forget the former things; do not
> dwell on the past. See, I am doing a new
> thing! (Isaiah 43:18–19)

I hear people say all the time, "Forget about your past." I totally disagree, because if you forget about your past, you will forget how far you have come. Here is an example: If you were a recovering drug addict and you forgot about your dangerous past, you wouldn't be able to be a testimony to those who want to recover, but they just needed to see someone who has made it. Another example: If you were molested as a child, when you became an adult, you didn't let whatever happened to you control you. But if you forgot about that painful and hurtful past, how can you help someone who went or who's going through the same painful things?

The list can go on and on. When you become a Christian, there is a place where there will be no more pain. There is a place where all old things have passed away.

> He will wipe every tear from their
> eyes. There will be no more deaths or
> mourning or crying or pain, for the
> old order of things has passed away.
> (Revelation 21:4)

No matter what pain, sorrow, sufferings, or hurt that you are going through, God has the last word. He writes the final chapter.

The Closing Statement for Inmates in the State and Federal Prisons

This is something I put together for the people who can't stay out of prison. It is not worth your life to be locked up behind bars. It is not worth your life to be doing the crimes that you do. Now, don't get me wrong, I'm not judging you; but it's just not worth it. Maybe your father and mother walked out on when you were just a child, or your mother was on drugs, and you probably felt alone all your life.

Whatever the case may be, we are responsible for our own actions, not the system. We can't blame the white man or the black man, and we can't even blame God who allows it to happen to us. We come to prison because of our own evil desires. It's just not worth it when people tell you when to eat, when to sleep, and when to take a shower. Do you like your life like that?

It's just not worth your life. God has a plan for every one of us, and I know it's not behind bars. We are so caught up into this world that we forget who we are and where we come from. We can call ourselves thugs, gangsters, players, and pimps; but when it comes down to it, we are nobody without Christ.

We are allowing our children to see us in and out of prison like a grocery store. Is this a message we want to send to our kids? So stay *out* of prison and stop doing the things that bring us to prison. We want to get mad at the officers because they're taking stuff from us. Well, stay *out* and you won't have to worry about that problem.

Don't get mad at me. I'm just keepin' it real! Since I've been in prison, I've learned a lot of good and bad things. This is not the place to be, and this is not the place to die and wonder if God forgave you and if your soul has been set free.

If you feel like you're about to fall, pray and ask God for wisdom, faith, strength, and peace. Read his Word to guide you. Everything you go through is in God's Word, and it teaches you how to get through it. Brothers and sisters, whatever you do, try to make the world a better place, and just *stay out*!

CHAPTER 29

It's All in My Head

Listen,
These are the things I see.
These are the things that are destroying
    me.
But what I can't figure out is, how did all
    this come about?
One day I'm fine.
The next day I'm doing time.
Damn!
Ain't life a b———h?
So, I thought like a rash or an itch.
Now that I'm in the position to be
    poisoned.
Evil is all around, it's up and it's down.
I try not to have fear,
But the presence of my enemies is near.
I try not to have those evil desires.
But the closer I get I feel like I'm burning
    in hell's everlasting fire.
My strength is gone.
I feel like I'm all alone.
My soul is trying to escape to a better
    place.

Is there a way that I can see Jesus's face?
Something inside of me is tearing me
apart.
Rescue me from the fire of death.
Get me in time so I have the piece of my
life back.
What's left?
But there's one thing this was nothing
but a dream.
I don't know what it means, but it's all in
my head.
Did you hear what I said?
It's all in my head,
And soon one day the nightmares will be
dead.

Shine on Me

As I sit here in prison
Trying to make a decision,
As I looked back over my life,
I thank God for Jesus Christ.
I could have been dead,
But instead, I'm alive and well.
One, two, five, or six years,
It seems like a lot, but it's not.
I'm still getting my blessings
As God teaches me a lesson.
There've been times that I've been
depressed
And thought of myself as less.
As you read God's Word,

I know that I can receive God's helping
    hand.
My enemies tried to hold me down,
But my soul just got found.
They tried to put me away,
But I'm still making it
Each and every day.
They tried to break me,
But it wasn't God's destiny.
Nope, not today!
Can't nobody make me,
Because I'm shielded by God's glory.
It's time to take a stand,
Because I know I can.
It's time for me to be set free.
So, Lord,
Shine on me!

A New Walk, "My Vision"

In 2014, there are things I haven't seen.
They open the doors and now I'm free.
I still can't believe this has happened to me.
Out with the old and in with the new.
My life is changing all the way through.
But now that I'm out, I will leave the past
    in the past.
It's time to start a new beginning because
    the old didn't last.
My family and friends, they stayed with
    me until the end.
And this is the love that God gave from
    up above.

This is a new walk along with a new talk.
The old me is gone, and I'm not doing
    this alone
Praises to Thee,
That gave me the right key to be free.
My eyes are open, and my ears can hear.
I don't think I have any more fears,
Not even a single tear.
I'm walking out tall and strong,
So, don't try to stop me because you'll be
    wrong.
There's no need for me to cry
Because I've been saved from the Lord
    Most High.
Now this is the end of my vision.
It's time for me to make the right decision.
This is my new walk!

My Name Is Resurrection

The first day, I'm dead.
The second day, I'm still dead,
But on the third day, I arise from death.
My life has been revived.
You thought I was dead,
But instead, I was restoring myself to be
    a better me.
You tried to make me blind where I
    couldn't see.
You thought I was lost, which I was,
But now I'm found, coming back to life
    safe and sound.

You had officers to arrest me and put me
      in a place of darkness.
Nevertheless, I thought my so-called
      friends will never betray me.
Now you're denying me, doubting me,
      and even insulting me.
They wanted me to stand before the
      world,
I'm talking about every last boy and girl.
Some wanted me free
And most turn their backs on me.
I'm sentenced to death.
You know, it's funny, they did the same
      thing to Jesus.
They hung him high on the cross.
They thought his soul was lost.
He could have fought back, but he just let
      them attack.
He could have saved himself,
But if he did, we as people wouldn't have
      anything left.
Jesus was crucified as the people watched
      him suffer in pain
Because all they wanted was the fame.
Christ asked God the Father to forgive
      us just because he loved us so much.
Even though the people lied, now Christ
      hung his head and died.
So, they put him in a tomb so his body
      can rest.
The guards were guarding him,
Guarding Christ like he was a pest.
The first day past,

Christ was dead. Even on the second day,
Christ was still dead.
But early Sunday morning on the third
        day,
God opened up the heavens
And Christ,
Jesus Christ, that is,
Arose just like he said he would do
To help us and bring us through. God
        gave me the power to follow Christ
And to do right in my life.
People thought my soul was dead,
But what God did for Christ, Christ did
        for me.
He raised me and revived me
And made me hold again. Jesus picked
        me up from the ground
With all power in his hand.
Now, I'm walking around in nothing but
        white.
Jesus is shining on me along with his
        spiritual light.
As for the people who crucified me
And left me in the world to die.
You are being forgiven by me
And the Lord Most High.
But I just want you to know,
My earthly name is Joshua Keith
        Roberson.
But my spiritual name is,
Because I was dead
And now I'm alive.
My name is Resurrection!

WORDS OF ENCOURAGEMENT

Don't be stuck in the past. That is exactly what the devil wants you to do. We can recover from our past, and God will even work good out of it. God is a redeemer. But God is a forgiving God. I challenge you today to start saying, "I am forgiven, God has a good plan for my life, and I will never look back and dwell on my past. But I will use my past to be my testimony for today." If we are supposed to look back, we would have eyes in the back of our heads, but we don't, so we should always look forward. Don't spend time bowing down to carnal thoughts and feelings. It is time to live deeper than the soul (mind, will, and emotions). It is time to believe we are joint heirs with Jesus Christ and that we can reign as kings in life through righteousness. Read Romans 5:17, 8:17.

God always gives us everything we need to enable us to be victorious in life, and he has given us what we need to defeat Satan. Words are powerful especially negative ones. Start using positive words of what God has promised you.

I am a new creature in Christ, old things have passed away. (2 Corinthians 5:17)

I cast all my cares upon him, he cares for me. (1 Peter 5:7)

I do not fear, I do not feel guilty, or condemned. (1 John 4:18)

No weapon formed against me shell prosper. (Isaiah 54:17)

We are told to read God's Word and meditate on the precepts of God. Listen carefully, you can bless or curse your future with the power of the tongue. Are there dreams you would like to happen or do you have a vision that enables your words to align with it?

Stop worrying about people who say negative things about what you used to do in the past or think less of you in your past. You can defeat your enemies by trusting God. Stay strong through the storms of life.

When the world says, "Give up," hope whispers, "Give it one more try." So it's time to change your words, to change your life, and to be set free, because the devil is a liar.

www.ingramcontent.com/pod-product-compliance
Lightning Source LLC
Chambersburg PA
CBHW031310160726
47993CB00001B/357